Wealth Wisdoms

For The Modern Financial Landscape

Dr. Andreas Svoboda

Copyright © 2023 by Andreas Svoboda

Disclaimer

This eBook is for informational purposes only. The author is not an expert in the fields discussed and the information presented should not be considered as professional advice. Use the information in this eBook at your own risk.

I have tried to make sure the info is accurate, but I can't promise it is perfect. I am not responsible for any errors or results that come from using this information.

You can't copy or share this eBook without the author's permission.

About Author

Andreas Svoboda stands as a distinguished figure in the spheres of finance, insurance, and academia. Presently, he holds esteemed positions as a Professor at the United International Business Schools in Zurich, and as the Head of Finance and Leadership, Banking and Finance at the Swiss Distance University of Applied Sciences (FFHS). Beyond his academic roles, Andreas is the visionary behind THE Insurance Academy and Vision Goal LLC, showcasing his keen entrepreneurial flair.

With an illustrious career in finance, he possesses advanced qualifications such as an LL.M. in International Business Law and a Doctor of Business Administration. His proficiency is further accentuated by his multilingual capabilities, diverse publications, and prominent certifications including the Certified Financial Planner (CFP®). Through 'Svoboda Finance' on YouTube, Andreas extends his wealth of knowledge, illuminating the path to financial literacy for many.

Table of contents

Introduction

The financial world saw significant changes in the second half of the twentieth century. The financial markets of the time were experiencing a transformation, housing bubbles had yet to break, and the globe had not yet seen the consequences of global recessions. The typical person's approach to wealth development and financial education was much different back then than it is now. "Rich Dad, Poor Dad," published in 1997, served as a guiding light for many readers, exposing them to the fundamental ideals of financial independence and the significance of financial education. It explained the differences between assets and liabilities in layman's terms and emphasized the significance of prudent investing and diversifying income sources.

As influential as the original book was in molding its readers' financial mindsets, the turn of the century brought unprecedented improvements, spurred principally by the digital revolution. The rise of the internet changed the global scene, democratizing knowledge and providing technologies previously only available to financial elites. From cryptocurrencies that challenge our conventional concept of cash to robo-advisors that make investing accessible to everybody, the barriers to entry into the financial world have been significantly reduced.

However, with these achievements come complications. Derivatives, ETFs, and other types of financial instruments have emerged, further complicating the investing environment. Navigating this demands not just reading, but also a profound knowledge and the capacity to quickly adapt to shifting tides.

Furthermore, the sources of our income have experienced drastic upheaval. While the typical 9-to-5 job is still widespread, it is no longer the sole viable way to generate income. From online business to content production and involvement in the developing gig economy, the digital era provides a myriad of alternatives.

Real estate, a cornerstone of Kiyosaki's ideas, has not been spared from current innovations. Property management is rapidly becoming tech-enhanced, and short-term rentals driven by platforms like Airbnb provide new income streams. Furthermore, property crowdfunding has provided a collaborative approach to real estate investing, enabling anyone to participate in property ownership without large cash outlays.

However, the essence stays the same. The mentality of constant learning, adaptation, and a thorough grasp of financial mechanics is as relevant today as it was decades ago. This book seeks to bridge the gap between historical knowledge and contemporary advances. We may construct a road to financial success in today's volatile terrain by learning historical ideas and applying them to our present circumstances.

The first chapter, "Technological Impact on Finance," will dive deeply into technology's transformational effect on the financial industry. We will track the growth of financial technology from the early days of digital banking to today's modern FinTech solutions. As we go further, readers will learn how internet platforms, robo-advisors, and cutting-edge applications have altered investing processes and made them more accessible to the general public.

The second chapter, "Investment Landscape," examines the significant changes in how individuals invest. We contrast classic investing paths with their contemporary equivalents, focusing light on the plethora of options open to today's investors. The realm of digital assets, such as cryptocurrencies, which have ushered in a new age of decentralized finance, will get special emphasis.

Our third chapter, "Understanding Financial Complexity," takes a deep dive into the complexities of contemporary finance. Understanding the market's plethora of financial products, ranging from ETFs to derivatives, becomes critical. We will dissect these instruments, explaining confusing jargon and providing self-education strategies to empower the contemporary investor.

"The Psychology of Money," the fourth chapter, delves into the human aspect of money. Our financial choices are both emotional and intellectual. We dissect the numerous emotions at work, from the fear of losing out to the underlying greed that sometimes governs investing decisions. We also discuss scarcity and abundance mindsets in this investigation, underlining their enormous influence on one's financial path.

Our fifth chapter, "Managing Emotions in Finances," emphasizes the role of emotional intelligence in financial decision-making. We talk about the necessity of defining financial goals, the function of budgeting, and how automation in savings may help with wealth growth. We'll also discuss when and why someone should consider getting professional financial aid.

In our sixth chapter, "Diversifying Income Streams," we go through the age-old adage of avoiding placing all of your eggs in one basket. The baskets, on the other hand, have developed. We'll look at current revenue sources, such as the gig economy and internet business, and evaluate their possibilities and limitations in today's society.

"Modern Real Estate Insights," Chapter 7, returns to the subject of property investing, which was a cornerstone of Kiyosaki's earlier teachings. However, with new trends such as short-term rentals, property crowdfunding, and technology-driven property management emerging, a lot has changed, and we will cover these movements thoroughly.

"Continuous Learning in Finance," our final chapter, underlines the ever-changing character of finance. With the financial sector in continual motion, the concept of continuous learning has never been more important. We'll go through resources, tools, and techniques for staying current, as well as the necessity of adaptation in attaining financial success.

In "Success Stories," we tell the true stories of those who have successfully navigated the new financial world. Analyzing the methods of people like Jeff Bezos, Mark Zuckerberg, Elon Musk, and Riccardo Salinas Pliego will give readers not just inspiration but also concrete lessons that they can use for their own financial adventures.

Chapter 1

Technological Impact on Finance

The current financial environment is constantly changing, owing mostly to fast technology breakthroughs. The reach of technology has permeated every aspect of finance, fundamentally affecting how people and institutions approach money management, investing, and wealth generation.

To begin with, technology has leveled the playing field. Deep financial expertise and resources were once the realm of a privileged few. With the internet and cell phones' pervasiveness, massive troves of financial information and tools are now only a click away. This democratization has resulted in a new generation of financially educated and empowered people willing to take charge of their financial fate.

Furthermore, the emergence of FinTech — the use of technology in financial services - has transformed how we handle and interact with money. Traditional banking institutions, traditionally defined by physical branches and paperwork, are increasingly being challenged by online-only digital banks. From simple savings and checking accounts to complicated financial products, these organizations provide customers with quick, smooth, and frequently less-priced services.

Investing has also been altered. Individuals no longer need large quantities to begin investing thanks to the rise of robo-advisors. These automated systems, which are driven by complicated algorithms, provide tailored investing advice, enabling even people with little resources to develop varied portfolios. This automation is a long cry from the days when starting a business required substantial funds and the services of a stockbroker.

The growth of cryptocurrencies and blockchain technology is another key trend. Bitcoin and other digital currencies represent a fundamental change in our concept of money. They exist outside of regular financial institutions and provide a decentralized means of transaction. While they are risky and volatile, their potential as an alternative asset class cannot be overlooked. Understanding their complexities and possibilities is becoming an essential aspect of current financial discourse.

Furthermore, the gig economy, which is powered by platforms such as Uber, Airbnb, and countless freelance sites, introduces new possibilities and concerns. Individuals may monetize their talents or assets using technological platforms, providing flexible work choices. However, typical financial safety nets, such as pensions or employer-provided health insurance, may be lacking. Navigating this new financial world requires a new financial viewpoint.

The pervasiveness of technology in finance is clear. It provides tremendous prospects while also necessitating a new degree of financial understanding. The contemporary person must be nimble, knowledgeable, and proactive, ready to exploit technology tools while also protecting themselves from possible hazards. One thing is certain as the financial world continues to evolve technologically: those who adapt and educate themselves will be best positioned to flourish.

The rise of FinTech: Its implications and opportunities.

The Democratization of Financial Tools

The emergence of FinTech has caused a seismic change in finance during the past several decades. The principle of decentralization is key to this movement. Financial institutions no longer have a monopoly on financial tools and services. Because of FinTech, anybody with a smartphone or computer may now access financial services from anywhere in the globe.

This democratization movement started with Internet banking, which allowed consumers to monitor their accounts and conduct transactions without having to visit a physical branch. It grew fast with the emergence of robo-advisors, which are platforms that provide automated investing advice based on algorithms. Individuals with little experience or resources may now easily join the financial sector thanks to such platforms.

Peer-to-peer lending platforms have also emerged, posing a threat to established lending institutions. These platforms link lenders and borrowers directly, eliminating the need for middlemen and frequently giving more affordable rates.

This has far-reaching consequences. Individuals have a greater duty to handle their funds responsibly as financial instruments become more accessible. While in the past, individuals depended on financial counselors or bankers for help, today's contemporary person must be proactive in learning and using the myriad of instruments accessible.

Emerging Economies and FinTech:

Another game-changing characteristic of FinTech is its ability to close the economic gap in developing nations. Historically, large segments of developing-country populations have been excluded from official financial institutions owing to a lack of infrastructure, paperwork, or resources. FinTech applications and platforms, on the other hand, are closing this gap by offering alternative banking, lending, and investing options.

In regions of Africa, for example, mobile money systems have witnessed phenomenal development, enabling users to save and transfer money using just their cell phones. Such innovations not only provide financial inclusion but also pave the road for developing economies to overtake established banking institutions.

Furthermore, by concentrating on certain sectors, such as agricultural financing or microloans, FinTech businesses are filling holes left by conventional banks. They are thereby strengthening previously disadvantaged groups and creating new economic prospects.

However, as much as FinTech provides opportunities, it also presents obstacles. Because of regulatory obstacles, worries about data privacy, and the potential for abuse, we must be cautious as we adopt these new technologies. This new financial world needs comprehensive knowledge, stressing both the benefits and the problems it provides.

FinTech's emergence is altering the global financial environment in new ways. As we navigate this contemporary financial age, armed with cutting-edge technologies at our disposal, it is critical to comprehend, adapt, and make educated decisions. In the words of the original "Rich Dad, Poor Dad," the onus is now more than ever on us to be informed and proactive in our financial path.

Adapting to the Evolving Real Estate Landscape

Real estate, a cornerstone of Kiyosaki's ideas, is still an important wealth-building vehicle, but its dynamics have changed substantially since the late 1990s. While the fundamental concepts of location and value remain important, technological advances have brought new trends and techniques to the real estate world.

Platforms such as Airbnb have transformed the notion of property rentals. Instead of typical long-term leases, property owners may now explore short-term rentals, which generally result in better profits. This strategy, however, comes with its own set of issues, such as increased wear and tear, frequent tenant rotations, and variable rental restrictions in various jurisdictions.

Property crowdfunding systems have arisen in the investing space, enabling people to participate in real estate with lower quantities than were previously necessary. Because of the democratization of real estate investing, a larger audience may profit from property appreciation and rental revenues.

Furthermore, technological advancements have improved the efficiency of property administration. Landlords and property managers are more prepared than ever to manage their properties, thanks to smart home devices that improve tenant experiences and platforms that automate rent collection and maintenance requests.

However, as technology is integrated into the real estate industry, it becomes increasingly vulnerable to global trends. For example, the post-pandemic boom in distant employment has affected property values in both urban and rural locations. Navigating contemporary real estate, like other financial arenas, requires a mastery of both classic concepts and cutting-edge tendencies.

The financial teachings from "Rich Dad, Poor Dad" are still relevant today, albeit in a very different context. Understanding and adjusting to these recent changes is critical for financial success in today's environment.

Navigating the Cryptocurrency Conundrum:

Cryptocurrencies, formerly considered a fringe notion, have infiltrated mainstream financial conversation. The advent of Bitcoin called "digital gold," signaled the start of a larger investigation into the worlds of decentralized finance and blockchain technology. The attractiveness of cryptocurrencies arises from their promise of financial independence, free of established banking institutions and government scrutiny.

With its smart contract features, Ethereum broadened the scope of what blockchain technology might do. These smart contracts opened the path for decentralized apps, transforming industries ranging from banking to entertainment. Then there's the larger crypto market, with altcoins catering to specific needs ranging from privacy-focused coins to those that assist the arts and entertainment industry.

Cryptocurrencies provide a unique opportunity for the contemporary investor. They provide a safeguard against conventional financial systems, particularly during times of economic turmoil. Furthermore, since these digital assets are decentralized, they are internationally accessible, enabling investing possibilities regardless of regional limits(Bilyk, 2023).

However, along with the gain comes the danger. The volatile nature of cryptocurrency values may result in large profits or substantial losses in a short period of time. There is also a learning curve connected with comprehending wallets, private keys, and the complexities of various blockchain systems.

In a world where digital assets are becoming as significant as conventional ones, it is critical to approach cryptocurrencies with a balanced mindset, appreciating both their promise and their drawbacks. It's not only about following the newest trend but also about understanding the underlying technology and its long-term repercussions.

Sustainable Finance and Environmental Responsibility

The environmental problems of the twenty-first century have refocused attention on sustainable finance. As people become more aware of climate change and its consequences, there is a greater focus on incorporating environmental, social, and governance (ESG) concerns into investment choices.

Modern businesses are judged not just on their revenue but also on their environmental and social effect. This transition is seen in the increase of green bonds, which support environmental initiatives, as well as the rising demand for ESG-focused mutual funds and ETFs.

The stock market is not the only source of sustainable funding. Green buildings, stressing energy efficiency, sustainable construction materials, and environmentally friendly designs, are also on the rise in the real estate market. Similarly, there is an increase in enterprises concentrating on sustainable solutions, from clean energy to waste management, in the startup environment.

This green transformation is a moral as well as an economic necessity. Companies that ignore sustainable practices put themselves in danger of regulatory fines, reputational harm, and a loss of confidence from both customers and investors.

Understanding the subtleties of sustainable finance is critical for the contemporary person navigating the financial world. It is about realizing that long-term financial prosperity is closely connected to environmental stewardship. In an age when the world is facing environmental issues, sustainable finance provides a way to guarantee that our financial activities contribute positively to the planet's future.

How online platforms, robo-advisors, and fintech apps have democratized investing

Transcending Traditional Monetary Systems

While Robert Kiyosaki previously revealed his two dads' opposing financial theories, today's world has a third participant - the digital domain. The rise of cryptocurrencies is at the vanguard of this digital frontier. This isn't meant to replace the tried-and-true strategy of prioritizing assets above obligations. Instead, it is about comprehending a whole new kind of asset.

Decades ago, the concept of digital, decentralized money seemed nearly absurd. Nonetheless, Bitcoin, Ethereum, and a slew of other cryptocurrencies are generating headlines. These are not simply currencies; they are declarations of financial insurrection. For many people, cryptocurrencies symbolize a newfound independence from centralized financial institutions, allowing them to conduct cross-border transactions without the need for conventional banking middlemen or currency conversions.

The underlying technology - blockchain - is what makes these digital currencies so appealing. Blockchain, a decentralized ledger system, offers security and integrity, attributes traditionally associated with conventional financial institutions. Blockchain, on the other hand, functions beyond boundaries, making it a genuinely global entity.

Understanding and investing in cryptocurrency involves more than simply following a trend. It is about understanding the larger trend of decentralization and the empowerment of individual investors. While the volatility of these digital currencies might be intimidating, the potential for innovation and development is also. After all, each asset, whether digital or physical, comes with its own set of difficulties and possibilities.

Embracing New Income Streams:

In the original "Rich Dad, Poor Dad," the notion of employment was centered on regular occupations or developing brick-and-mortar enterprises. However, the internet has changed our perception of labor and, by extension, money generation.

Consider the generation of content. Artists, educators, entertainers, and influencers may now monetize their hobbies thanks to platforms like YouTube, Twitch, and Patreon. These platforms are more than just entertainment channels. They reflect the democratization of content, with community interaction and true talent driving value rather than large-scale production firms.

Similarly, the gig economy has grown, signaling a trend away from traditional 9-to-5 occupations and toward more flexible, project-based positions. Upwork, Fiverr, and Freelancer have evolved into global marketplaces, connecting qualified people with customers from all around the globe. Geographic barriers dissolve in this environment, and abilities take center stage.

This digital transformation is not without its difficulties. Because of the intermittent nature of online revenue and the competitive market, consistency may be difficult. However, the benefits, both financially and personally, may be enormous for those who traverse this arena with expertise and determination.

The methods to acquire assets and liabilities have grown in a world where the definition of assets and obligations has expanded. Today's financial ecosystem provides several possibilities for individuals eager to study, adapt, and create, whether it's through delving into the depths of digital currencies or utilizing the power of internet platforms.

Beyond Traditional Banking

In a world where financial literacy is essential, the rise of decentralized finance, often known as DeFi, has added a new chapter to the contemporary financial playbook. DeFi is a technology that makes financial goods accessible on a public decentralized blockchain network, allowing anybody to utilize them without the need for middlemen. It calls into question the basic foundations of conventional banking by proposing a system in which users have total control over their assets and transactions.

The consequences of DeFi are enormous. Consider collecting income on your money without using a bank or borrowing without requiring clearance from a financial organization. When criteria are satisfied, smart contracts on blockchain platforms automatically execute these agreements, minimizing the need for middlemen and, as a result, costs.

However, with such independence comes responsibility. Individuals are completely accountable for their financial actions in the DeFi area since banks do not serve as a middleman or provide deposit protection. This needs a thorough grasp of the platforms and instruments used, underscoring the significance of financial education in today's complicated world once again.

However, DeFi's attraction is inescapable. It offers a future with more inclusive, efficient, and transparent financial systems. It's a world full of opportunities for the savvy investor or user, but it also emphasizes the significance of caution and ongoing learning in our fast-changing financial climate.

Digital Wallets and Seamless Transactions:

The entire way we handle and transmit money has changed dramatically. Cash and cheques are no longer the exclusive means of financial transactions. Today, the power of technology has given rise to digital wallets, ushering in a new age of ease and security.

Digital wallets, often known as e-wallets, are more than simply a virtual money storage facility. They are a unified platform via which consumers may manage different bank accounts, credit cards, and even loyalty points. E-wallets have altered the financial experience for customers, whether it's paying for groceries with a phone touch or sending money across continents in seconds (What Is the Impact of Technology on Financial Services? | HCLTech, 2021).

The universal popularity of digital wallets has also facilitated financial inclusion. E-wallets offer the public a conduit to the digital economy in many locations where conventional banking systems are few or unavailable. People may now trade, save, and even invest without relying on traditional banks.

However, obstacles remain, as with all digital breakthroughs. Data security, privacy, and possible system vulnerabilities are all common concerns. As a result, users must not only appreciate the conveniences provided by digital wallets but also be aware of best practices for safeguarding their assets and personal information. Understanding the complexities of digital wallets will be a cornerstone of contemporary financial literacy as we move toward a paperless future.

Chapter 2

Investment Landscape

The spheres of investment have grown, shifted, and become more complicated than they were in the past as a result of the dynamic nature of the modern world. Several decades ago, the most common types of investments, such as stocks, bonds, and real estate, were the most popular options. However, as we go farther into the 21st century, a variety of fresher, more diversified, and more complicated investment opportunities call out to the smart investor.

First and foremost, it is very necessary to acknowledge the pervasive impact of the internet. The barriers to entry into the stock market have been dramatically reduced because of the proliferation of Internet trading platforms and real-time financial news. A person may now get started without having to have significant financial resources or a personal broker. One has the ability to acquire fractional shares, have rapid access to overseas markets, and make educated judgments based on data that is updated in real-time.

In a similar vein, the field of real estate has seen substantial changes during the last several decades. The days are far gone when all that was involved in real estate transactions was the purchase of a home or a plot of land. Individuals are now able to participate in portfolios of real estate assets without owning actual properties because of the advent of real estate investment trusts (REITs), which were made possible by the digital age and its attendant developments. Crowdfunding platforms that specialize in real estate, on the other hand, make it possible for investors to combine their resources in order to support certain projects. This provides investors with the opportunity to make a return without requiring an initial investment of a significant amount of money.

The investing ecosystem now has additional layers of complexity as a result of the introduction of derivatives and exchange-traded funds (ETFs). Without having to make a direct investment in the underlying asset, investors may nevertheless obtain exposure to certain industries or commodities, hedge against potential losses, and speculate on the direction of future prices thanks to a variety of financial instruments. They have their own particular hazards in addition to the enhanced potential for earnings that they provide, which highlights the critical need to have a solid understanding of personal finance in this day and age.

The ascent of cryptocurrencies has also been dramatic in recent years. Investing in digital currency, such as Bitcoin and Ethereum, presents investors with a whole new set of challenges and opportunities. Blockchain technology, which underpins cryptocurrencies like Bitcoin and Ethereum, has the potential to shake up a wide range of industries, from banking to the management of supply chains. Despite the fact that their volatility is noticeable, the potential return is just too significant to ignore.

In addition, the advent of the internet era has made it possible for non-traditional investing platforms to emerge, such as those that specialize in rare collectibles, art, or even shoes as investments. These alternate investment routes, which are made possible by the connecting power of the internet, emphasize the many options that are open to the contemporary investor.

On the other hand, with great potential comes even greater responsibility. Due to the scope and complexity of the current financial world, investors need to exercise extreme caution, continue their education, and be flexible. It is not enough to just have access to money; one must also be aware of when, when, and how to put it to use. A well-informed and strategic approach, together with a voracious appetite for information, will be the defining characteristics that differentiate successful investors of today from those who are falling further and more behind. One thing is abundantly evident as the environment continues to change, and that is the fact that investing is no longer a luxury enjoyed by a select few but rather a need shared by the many. Investing is essential to obtaining financial independence and long-term prosperity.

Traditional vs. Modern investment avenues.

Navigating the Cryptocurrency Wave:

As we make our way through the modern panorama of financial opportunities, we cannot ignore the transformation brought on by digital currencies. The emergence of cryptocurrencies as a formidable asset class, with Bitcoin at the forefront of this trend, has posed a challenge to conventional financial institutions and presented an altogether novel approach to the concept of wealth and value.

Cryptocurrencies, at their foundation, are decentralized ledger systems, which renders them resistant to the regulatory oversight exercised by centralized authorities. This essential character of theirs offers them both advantages and disadvantages. On the one hand, they offer to democratize financial power by allowing users to circumvent existing banking institutions. This would allow users to benefit from possibly cheaper transaction costs and greater degrees of anonymity. On the other hand, due to the absence of any kind of centralized supervision, the cryptocurrency market is famously volatile, and its values are prone to making significant movements within a very short amount of time.

Cryptocurrencies, on the other hand, provide a mix of enormous promise and big risk for an investor with discernment. Due to the fact that they are decentralized, they are protected to some extent from traditional economic downturns. Additionally, their scarcity, particularly in the case of Bitcoin, might cause their value to increase. However, because of the newness of the market, it is susceptible to being impacted by a variety of factors, including speculation, technology advancements, and regulatory news, which makes it unpredictable.

It is essential to have a comprehensive knowledge of the technology behind cryptocurrencies as well as an accurate estimate of the level of risk one is willing to take before making any judgments in this space. Even while the possibility of exponential profits could be enticing, it is essential to be aware that, as with any other investment, there is always the possibility of incurring significant losses.

The Gig Economy and Freelance Investments:

In today's complex financial environment, it is not enough to just know where to put one's money; one must also understand how to make money. The proliferation of the gig economy and chances for freelance work, which has been spurred by websites such as Uber, Airbnb, and Upwork, has provided people with a wide variety of channels via which they may diversify their sources of income.

These platforms have brought about a significant paradigm change in the work landscape. People now have the ability to give their talents, assets, or services on a project or "gig" basis, and they may often have flexibility in terms of both their time commitment and their level of dedication. This concept gives many people the opportunity to profit from their unique abilities or assets that aren't being used to their full potential, which might result in huge financial gains.

However, however liberating the gig economy may seem to be, it also introduces new financial complications. Freelancers often face the challenge of managing their personal finances autonomously, including their taxes, health insurance, and retirement plans, due to the unpredictability of their income. It is possible to reduce certain risks by spreading your activities among a number of different platforms or jobs, but doing so requires skilled financial management.

Understanding the intricacies of self-employment, such as the tax ramifications and the need to set up an emergency fund, is very necessary for those who are considering venturing into this sector. The spirit of the contemporary investment landscape may be seen exemplified in the spirit of the gig economy, which, in all its splendor, represents the spirit of the current investment landscape. The modern investing landscape is rife with possibilities, but success requires vigilance, adaptation, and an unyielding dedication to financial education.

Simplifying Complex Investment Structures

ETFs, or exchange-traded funds, have seen a meteoric rise in popularity among contemporary investors. ETF is an abbreviation for exchange-traded funds. ETFs are not restricted to a single stock, bond, or commodity; rather, they provide a composite basket that enables investors to diversify their holdings within a particular market specialty or across wide industries. Not only does this diversification contribute to their attraction, but so does the fact that they are simple to trade and closely resemble individual equities on the market.

Historically, investors seeking diversity have traditionally turned to mutual funds as their investment vehicle of choice. ETFs, on the other hand, have price changes that occur in real-time, which provides for more transparency than mutual funds, which only compute their Net Asset Value (NAV) once at the conclusion of each trading day. The flexibility to purchase or sell exchange-traded funds (ETFs) during trading hours, in combination with the fact that fee ratios for ETFs are often lower than those of mutual funds, has made them an appealing option for investors of all experience levels.

However, as the market for ETFs continues to expand, investors now have access to a variety of options, each of which is geared toward a certain industry, commodity, or investing strategy. The abundance of alternatives available to investors, while providing them with freedom, also requires that they have a deep grasp of the underlying assets and the patterns in the market. In addition, the simplicity of trading ETFs may often be a double-edged sword, as it can lead to rash judgments over whether to purchase or sell a certain security.

Therefore, investors need to approach exchange-traded funds (ETFs) with a balanced viewpoint. Not only is it essential to recognize their potential for widespread market exposure, but it is also essential to comprehend their complexities. In the ever-shifting terrain of contemporary finance, where possibilities abound, it is of the utmost importance to maintain a strong foundation in the principles of informed decision-making.

Digital Entrepreneurship:

The digital environment has morphed into a vast arena in which business initiatives may take place. The proliferation of highly effective tools, platforms, and technologies has resulted in a lowering of entry barriers, making it possible for a far wider variety of people to realize their dreams of starting their own businesses.

E-commerce platforms, for example, make it possible for anybody with an idea to open a storefront, allowing them to sell their wares to customers all over the world while avoiding the overhead costs associated with conventional storefronts. In a similar vein, platforms for content production, such as YouTube and Medium, provide users with options through which they may monetize their creativity, knowledge, or experiences. The digital economy has, in essence, made the accumulation of wealth more accessible to more people.

However, the fact that more people have access to information does not mean that success is automatically assured. The market for attention, consumers, and subscribers is very competitive in the Internet world since millions of people are competing for it. It takes more than simply an engaging product or content to be successful in digital business; you also need savvy marketing methods, an awareness of digital analytics, and, most importantly, tenacity.

Learning is something that should never stop for individuals who are interested in entering this field. Because of the fast evolution of digital tools and platforms and the shifting tastes of consumers, what is effective now may not be relevant tomorrow. To successfully navigate this ever-changing terrain, one must combine a strong sense of passion and flexibility with a dogged determination to acquire an awareness of the always-shifting digital pulse. The road of digital entrepreneurship, just like the journey of any other business, is full of obstacles, but the benefits may be enormous for those who are prepared to persist through them.

Choosing investments according to individual needs.

Navigating the Nuances of Short-term Investment Opportunities

The rise of the gig economy in the wake of our quickly advancing digital era brings an interesting new feature to the landscape of investing opportunities. They all exemplify the new work mindset where flexibility is valued more than longevity, whether they are Uber drivers, freelance writers, or hosts of short-term rental properties. But beyond its obvious consequences for employment, the gig economy has also given rise to new ideas on how money might be invested.

Throughout the course of economic history, the archetypal investor held down a conventional job, accumulated savings with the help of regular paychecks, and then placed those funds in standard investment vehicles. However, the terrain is far more diverse now than it was before. Gig workers need a unique approach due to the unpredictability of their revenue streams despite the fact that they are often profitable. Their inconsistent income may provide them with possibilities for making one-time investments, but it also requires them to adopt a more fluid strategy when it comes to making financial plans and taking financial risks.

It is critical for employees in today's contemporary economy to have an awareness of the ephemeral quality of their income and, as a result, of the need to establish an emergency savings cushion. In addition, despite the fact that they can be tempted by the promise of fast gains, it is essential for them to have a diversified investment portfolio that includes both risky and safe assets.

Moreover, since standard job benefits, such as retirement accounts, are not offered by gig economy employers, workers in this sector need to be proactive in their search for alternative methods of retirement savings. To ensure long-term financial stability, it is essential to make use of either self-employed pension plans or individual retirement accounts designed specifically for independent contractors.

Understanding these intricacies and consistently adjusting to the unpredictable nature of revenue from gigs will be essential for an ambitious investor coming from the arena of gigs. This will be the cornerstone of their investing path.

Harnessing Technology in Real Estate:

Even though it is sometimes referred to as an asset that will never become obsolete, real estate has not been immune to the profound technological shifts that have occurred in our time. Even while the essential assumption has not changed — that is, purchasing property with the intention of increasing its value — the methods have been subjected to significant change.

Potential investors are no longer limited to looking at local listings in newspapers or making time-consuming appointments with real estate agents. Platforms such as Zillow and Redfin make it possible for users to have instant access to detailed information on real estate markets all around the world. This not only makes access more democratic, but it also provides investors with data-driven insights that may help them make more educated choices.

Concurrently, the idea of ownership has developed further through time. People are able to make successful property investments with a small amount of funds via the use of property crowdfunding platforms, which also allows people to own fractions of several assets rather than a single property. This decentralized strategy lessens risks and provides exposure that is spread across a number of real estate markets.

Additionally, the traditionally difficult tasks of property care, tenant relations, and rent collecting are now simplified with the help of technology-augmented property management solutions. Investors now have the ability to manage their properties remotely, allowing them to maximize their earnings with a minimum of personal engagement.

However, there is a learning curve involved, as there is in any field that is driven by technology. It will be essential for contemporary real estate investors to master the art of adjusting to these new technologies, comprehending the complexities of using them, and maximizing their potential. Even while brick and mortar are still essential to the real estate industry in this digital era, screens, and software have emerged as indispensable partners for the industry.

The New Gold or a Modern Mirage?

When we go back to discussions about investments that took place in the latter part of the 20th century, we don't hear terminology like Bitcoin or Ethereum very often. However, in modern times, not only have they made their way into our vocabularies but also our financial portfolios. The tectonic transformations that have taken place in the current financial environment are best exemplified by cryptocurrencies, which are often hailed as the money of the future.

When they were first introduced, cryptocurrencies were considered to be on the periphery, a specialized topic of interest among lovers of technology. A fast forward to the present day reveals that they have developed into an important hub of the global financial system. These digital assets hold the promise of decentralization, provide an alternative to conventional financial systems, and embody the mindset of a generation that is distrustful of authorities in centralized positions of power.

On the other hand, great gains almost always come with significant dangers. It's common knowledge that cryptocurrencies are notoriously volatile. For example, Bitcoin has had parabolic gains followed by dramatic drops, all of which have occurred within very short timespans. Because of this unpredictability, investors need to be familiar with the dynamics of the market and have a risk appetite that allows them to tolerate the possibility of incurring losses.

In addition to the basic cryptocurrencies, the realm of decentralized finance (DeFi) and non-fungible tokens (NFTs) further broaden the scope of the possibilities. NFTs have fundamentally altered how we evaluate the worth of digital artwork and collectibles, while decentralized finance (DeFi) has the potential to re-create old financial institutions without the need for middlemen.

When it comes to investing, venturing into the world of cryptocurrencies is comparable to venturing into unknown seas. It is necessary to have knowledge of both technology concepts and market dynamics, but most importantly, one must be willing to acknowledge the immaturity and unpredictability of this asset class. It is a paradigmatic example of modern-day investment due to the enormous potential rewards as well as the enormous potential risks.

The rise of digital assets and cryptocurrencies.

Navigating the Globalized Nature of Digital Investment Platforms

During the time when the first edition of "Rich Dad Poor Dad" was published by Robert Kiyosaki, the international financial landscape was in disarray. The majority of investors were content to conduct their business inside the constraints of their own national markets, and institutional investors dominated the landscape of cross-border investment activity. Because of the expansion of digital platforms, the modern financial environment has evolved to provide consumers with unmatched access to investment possibilities all over the world. This is mostly due to the fact that digital platforms are more commonplace.

The elimination of geographical restrictions is one of the aspects of today's panorama of investment opportunities that stands out the most. It is possible to trade digital assets and cryptocurrencies in particular 24 hours a day, seven days a week, irrespective of national borders. A genuinely international market is shown by the fact that the same Bitcoin may be exchanged without any problems in New York, Tokyo, or Johannesburg.

Even more conventional asset types, such as stocks and bonds, have benefited from increased worldwide accessibility in recent years. These days, stock trading platforms provide an opportunity to invest in businesses located on several continents. It is now possible for a retail investor in Asia to hold shares in a fledgling company in Silicon Valley and for an investor in Europe to dip their toes into the booming IT industry in Africa. Both of these dreams have become a reality.

This process of globalization carries with it a multitude of benefits. Investing portfolios may be diversified not just across asset classes but also across regions, economies, and political landscapes if the investor so chooses. It provides them with options, enabling them to pursue opportunities in growing markets or hedge against economic uncertainty in their own countries. This gives them more power and empowers them with alternatives.

However, along with these benefits come their own special difficulties. To start, it might be challenging to comprehend the socio-economic and political complexities of other countries' marketplaces. A piece of technology that is considered to be ground-breaking in one region of the globe may be considered obsolete or even illegal in another. The potential of an investment may be affected by a number of factors, including local competition, regulatory positions, and market penetration dynamics.

In addition to that, there is the difficulty of different time zones. Because markets are open around the clock, big price swings may take place while an investor is sleeping, which might result in the investor missing out on opportunities or incurring losses they hadn't planned.

Alterations in the value of currencies also play an essential part. The relative value of an investor's native currency in comparison to the currency of the invested asset may have a major impact on the value of an investment. This can work either in the investor's favor or against them.

Investors need to take a more comprehensive strategy if they are going to successfully traverse the international digital investing market. This requires not just a comprehension of the fundamentals of the asset in which they are investing but also an awareness of the trends occurring on a worldwide scale. It means having a flexible attitude, an open mind, and, perhaps most significantly, having an insatiable curiosity. As boundaries continue to blur in the financial world, the investors who will prosper will be those who embrace global ideas while anchoring their plans in good investing concepts. Those who do not do so will be left behind.

The Evolution of Risk Management in Digital Asset Portfolios

Understanding the dangers that are involved with digital assets and cryptocurrencies and taking precautions against them has never been more important as the market for these assets continues to grow. In the conventional landscape of investments, risk management has developed over the course of centuries, with instruments and tactics that have been honed to perfection to shield investors from the volatility of the market. In contrast, the world of digital assets offers investors a whole new set of obstacles and uncertainties with which they must come to terms.

For example, the price of cryptocurrencies is notoriously difficult to predict. When compared to conventional assets, the elements that might significantly affect their price movements are often rather unique. Within a short period of time, price fluctuations may be caused by a variety of factors, including regulatory pronouncements, technical breakthroughs, and even trends on social media. This volatility may be a double-edged sword, resulting in either significant profit or significant losses depending on how it is used.

In addition, the fact that many digital assets are decentralized makes them susceptible to dangers that are associated with flaws in smart contracts or platform security. The responsibility for one's own safety and well-being must often be shouldered by the individual in a decentralized society, in contrast to conventional hierarchical structures, in which the culpable party is typically a centralized organization (Understanding the Investment Landscape | Quilter Cheviot, 2022). Because of this, there are now instances in which the loss of even a seemingly little mistake, such as misplacing a private key, may result in the irrevocable loss of cash.

In addition, the regulatory climate around digital assets is now in a state of upheaval. It is possible for policies to shift quickly, which may have an effect on investment plans, as governments and institutions all over the globe struggle to come to terms with the repercussions of this technology. For instance, the choice of a government to support digital assets or to restrict their use may have a significant impact on the adoption of these assets and, as a result, their value.

To be able to adjust to this ever-changing environment, risk management practices will need to be reevaluated. In the realm of digital assets, the concept of diversification, which is a cornerstone of conventional investment strategy, takes on new meanings and responsibilities. Investors may diversify their holdings not just among a variety of cryptocurrencies or tokens but also across a variety of blockchain ecosystems, use cases, or even consensus processes.

Continuous education and keeping up with the most recent developments in both technological and regulatory trends are very necessary. Investors need to be adaptable and able to adjust their tactics quickly in order to keep up with the fast speed of change that is occurring in the world of digital assets. The undertaking is difficult, but for those who are ready to traverse these intricacies, the world of digital assets provides prospects that are difficult to match in the conventional financial environment.

Chapter 3

Understanding Financial Complexity

Complexity has become both a difficulty and an opportunity in the developing world of finance. Today's financial landscape, with its plethora of various investment vehicles and unique financial products, needs a higher degree of comprehension. Understanding these complexities is not just a desirable characteristic but also a need for everyone seeking financial success in the current world.

Historically, financial tools were simple. The usual was a savings account, a fixed deposit, or a regular stock purchase. Today, we confront a plethora of possibilities, ranging from the complexities of cryptocurrency trading to the maze-like architecture of some derivatives. Navigating such possibilities takes judgment, expertise, and a need for lifelong learning.

The variety of financial instruments accessible adds to the complexity. Financial management tactics, tax consequences of diverse assets, and the interaction of global economic forces all add levels of complexity. Consider the worldwide consequences of currency trading or the hedging tactics used in commodities markets, for example. These aren't simply theoretical constructs; they're genuine tools that investors utilize on a daily basis.

But why is it critical to comprehend this complication? To begin with, understanding provides the capacity to make educated judgments. In a world brimming with financial possibilities, the astute investor can see the difference between a potentially profitable enterprise and a doubtful one. This awareness protects one from undue dangers while also providing doors to previously thought-inaccessible paths.

Furthermore, as the world becomes increasingly linked, the ripple effects of events in one part of the world may have a significant impact on markets in other parts of the world. Individuals who are financially knowledgeable and aware of these linkages may act ahead of time, altering their portfolio to prevent any negative consequences or capitalize on forthcoming possibilities.

Furthermore, as the digital age advances, disinformation and "financial myths" multiply at an alarming pace. Understanding financial complexity protects against falling victim to such fallacies, ensuring that one's financial path is founded on facts and good ideas.

The current financial tapestry, with its rich patterns and motifs, may seem intimidating to the untrained. However, the benefits are many for those willing to devote time and effort to deciphering its riddles. Passively saving and hoping for the best is no longer enough. The key to unlocking the jewels of today's economic world is active involvement driven by a thorough awareness of financial complexity. Accept complexity, comprehend its complexities, and allow it to steer you to a happy financial future.

Importance of financial literacy in a more complex system.

Deconstructing Financial Jargon for the Modern Investor

The jargon of contemporary finance seems to be expanding practically every day. Derivatives, ETFs, NFTs, and a plethora of other acronyms and terminology might be perplexing to the inexperienced. While the democratization of finance has been freeing, it has also produced a tangle of ideas that the average person may find difficult to understand. While many financial terminology existed during Kiyosaki's time, their ubiquity and direct influence on an individual's portfolio were not as evident as they are now.

The modern investor, whether a seasoned trader or a college student pondering their first stock purchase, must navigate through this vast and rather perplexing financial jargon. Understanding these words is essential not just for being familiar with money but also for making educated decisions. For example, stock traders might lose money if they do not understand the consequences of high-frequency trading or the mechanics of a short squeeze.

It is at this point that the significance of financial education becomes clear. Beyond just understanding what a phrase means, it is critical to comprehend its significance, consequences, and function in a wider financial plan. For many, the distinction between an ETF and a mutual fund or between a standard stock and a tokenized stock may seem insignificant. When it comes to investing and managing money, however, these discrepancies may have a significant influence on returns, risks, and portfolio balance.

In an age where financial blunders may be compounded by the quick movements of digital markets, understanding this growing lingo is not only useful but also critical. It serves as the cornerstone for strong, forward-thinking financial plans.

The Evolving Role of Financial Advisors in a Digital Age

There was a time when a financial advisor's function was obvious. They were the translators of the financial world, the link between sophisticated market dynamics and the general public. Their opinions, based on years of research and expertise, were often the main resource for those wishing to invest or manage their money. Robert Kiyosaki's initial universe was one in which these specialists were the gatekeepers of financial enlightenment.

In today's world, the terrain has changed. The internet, with its massive stores of data and democratized information, has helped to level the playing field to some degree. Investors now have tools that can auto-balance their portfolios, algorithms that forecast market changes, and platforms that provide quick peer assessments of financial strategy.

However, in this new era, the job of the human financial counselor has not been reduced; rather, it has evolved. While raw data and analytics may be obtained through digital platforms, nuanced understanding, personal touch, emotional intelligence, and ethical concerns remain firmly in the human sphere.

Modern financial counselors are more than simply information carriers. They are data translators who guide customers through the cacophony of internet information. They bring comfort in turbulent times, and maybe, most significantly, they provide perspective. In an era where data abounds but actual insight is few, their role in offering perspective, demystifying complicated techniques, and comprehending individual life objectives and anxieties remains vital.

It demonstrates the tenacity of human ties in money. While technologies and platforms advance, the need for trust, human connection, and nuanced knowledge in the financial sector remains consistent. Financial advisers continue to play an important part in the complicated dance of contemporary finance, harmonizing the beat between man and machine.

The Digital Revolution and Its Impact on Passive Income Streams

In the context of Robert Kiyosaki's original book, the concept of producing passive income was largely centered on real estate investments, stock dividends, and maybe intellectual property royalties. These ideas, although still important today, have been joined by a slew of new possibilities brought about by the digital revolution.

The digital revolution has not only changed how we interact, purchase, and consume information, but it has also changed how we earn. Websites, which were formerly considered digital brochures, have evolved into powerful revenue-generating tools. A well-maintained blog or specialty website may produce significant money from advertising, affiliate marketing, and sponsored content with the correct content strategy, SEO, and user interaction tools.

Online courses and e-books have also gained prominence. In today's environment, knowledge is a precious commodity. Experts in a variety of professions may now bundle and sell their knowledge to a worldwide audience without being limited by conventional publication or classroom restrictions. Platforms such as Udemy, Teachable, and Kindle Direct Publishing have democratized education and information sharing, enabling anyone to generate passive revenue from their ideas and abilities.

The growth of mobile applications and software-as-a-service (SaaS) platforms is another key change in the passive income space. Once produced and fine-tuned, digital tools and apps may function as recurring income sources with minimum post-development effort. The app economy provides a huge vista of potential for tech-savvy businesses, ranging from health monitors to productivity applications.

However, a consideration of digital passive revenue sources would be incomplete without the dynamic world of content production being acknowledged. Platforms such as

YouTube, Patreon, and Twitch have spawned a new breed of content producers that make passive income via subscriptions, ad revenue, and fan contributions. By continuously offering interesting material, these artists may build loyal fan communities and convert their passion projects into profitable businesses.

However, like with any financial venture, these internet routes have their own set of problems. Given the low entrance hurdles, competition is severe. Keeping up with ever-changing algorithms, preserving digital assets, and guaranteeing constant quality all need time and effort. Furthermore, the digital world is susceptible to economic swings, legislative shifts, and technical upheavals.

However, for those who are ready to adapt, learn, and endure, the digital world provides unrivaled prospects. It demonstrates how the essential ideas Kiyosaki emphasized — financial literacy, flexibility, and asset leveraging — remain ageless, even when the details of those assets and tactics change in response to technology improvements.

Breakdown of financial instruments: Derivatives, ETFs, algorithmic trading.

The Interconnected World of Global Finance:

As we dive further into the complexities of contemporary banking, it becomes clear that our global financial system is more intertwined than ever. The advent of new financial instruments has complicated the environment, but so has the way these instruments interact across various markets throughout the globe. Because of the globalization of finance, a glitch in one part of the world may send ripples throughout the world, impacting economies, businesses, and individual investors.

Previously, investing strategies might be essentially confined, focused on home markets with little exposure to global events. However, in today's interconnected world, it is critical to have a comprehensive awareness of global financial currents. For example, a Chinese economic slump may have an effect on the US IT sector, a political crisis in the Middle East can alter oil prices, influencing transportation costs globally, and a change in European Union policy might affect global trade dynamics.

But why is global interconnection so important for an individual investor? Because it emphasizes the significance of variety. Investors may diversify their risk across several locations and industries by using a variety of financial products, such as global ETFs, international bonds, and foreign shares. It also highlights the need for due diligence, which includes comprehending not just the instrument but also the larger economic and geopolitical issues that may impact it.

Furthermore, with technology playing such an important part in information distribution, global financial news moves at breakneck speed. Due to the real-time nature of financial data, investors must be flexible, discriminating, and well-informed. Algorithmic trading, which utilizes complicated mathematical models to make trading choices at breakneck rates, highlights the current financial world's pace.

However, additional complexity brings greater potential. Individuals may tap into growth stories from any area of the globe, hedge their risks more effectively, and possibly generate greater profits by harnessing the large pool of global resources, knowledge, and technologies accessible today. Indeed, the global financial network, with all of its complexities, invites the savvy investor eager to comprehend, adapt, and prosper within it.

Redefining Wealth in the Digital Age:

If there has been a significant movement in the perception of wealth over the last several decades, it has been the transition from primarily physical assets to a combination of tangible and intangible assets. While physical land, gold, and stocks remain mainstays of wealth, digital assets, intellectual property, internet presence, and personal brand are increasingly recognized as vital components of an individual's wealth.

Take a look at the emergence of influencers in the digital era. Their fortune is derived from their internet following, brand collaborations, and digital content rather than conventional assets. Similarly, today's companies are often valued not just on their physical assets but also on their user base, unique technology, and potential for disruption.

Cryptocurrencies, another digital-age phenomenon, challenge conventional conceptions of cash and wealth. Their worth is mostly determined by public opinion, technical trust, and adoption rates since they are not backed by any actual commodity or central authority.

Furthermore, as we transition to a more knowledge-based economy, intellectual assets such as patents, copyrights, and trademarks become increasingly important. Depending on its possible uses, a successful patent may be worth millions, if not billions, of dollars.

All of these changes point to a larger trend: wealth in the current era is complex. It's not simply about owning real estate or having money in the bank. It is about impact, creativity, adaptation, and the capacity to capitalize on the possibilities presented by the digital revolution. As we redefine wealth, we must also reconsider our tactics for accumulating, protecting, and growing it in this volatile environment.

Harnessing the Power of FinTech:

In today's volatile financial environment, the phrase "FinTech," short for financial technology, may seem to be a buzzword. Its ramifications and revolutionary potential, however, are apparent. FinTech has irreversibly impacted how we deal with money, from making stock trading accessible to the general public to expediting complicated banking operations.

The beginnings of FinTech may be traced back to the digitalization of banks in the late twentieth century. Nonetheless, the true boom began with the development of the internet and cell phones. What used to need a visit to a physical location - whether it was banking, investing, or even seeking financial guidance - became possible with a few clicks or taps.

Take a look at personal finance. Managing one's money used to include keeping physical ledgers or using primitive software. Modern applications not only monitor every cent and dollar but also give actionable insights planning tools, and even automate savings or investment. Individuals are empowered by such technologies, which enable them to be more proactive in their financial health without requiring much knowledge.

Similarly, internet platforms have democratized access to investing. Stock trading is no longer seen as a privilege of the wealthy. Anyone with access to the internet may now invest in a wide range of products, from standard equities to cutting-edge cryptocurrencies. These platforms often include research tools, tutorials, and even community conversations, allowing beginners to make educated selections.

However, arguably the most disruptive feature of FinTech is financial inclusion. Traditional banking systems, with their severe criteria, often left a sizable section of the world population unbanked or neglected. With their focus on accessibility and scalability, modern financial technologies are overcoming this gap. Digital wallets, peer-to-peer lending platforms, and even micro-investment applications are making crucial financial services available to more individuals than ever before.

However, such fast invention necessitates care. Because these technologies are digital in nature, cybersecurity is critical. Furthermore, the simplicity of usage may often lead to rash judgments, emphasizing the need for financial education.

In short, although FinTech has definitely made finance more accessible and efficient, it is critical to approach it with both excitement and caution. Individuals may actually harness the power of technology to improve their financial well-being by knowing and intelligently using these contemporary tools.

Tips for self-education on these instruments.

Ensuring Safe and Informed Investments

As the financial industry embraces the digital revolution, a plethora of platforms and services emerge on a daily basis, offering higher profits and simplicity of use. The digital era provides unparalleled access to a broad range of investing possibilities, from app-based stock trading platforms to cryptocurrency wallets. While this democratization has been mainly favorable, making educated decisions in the face of information overload may be difficult.

To begin, it is critical to assess the legitimacy of these sites. The temptation of rapid riches lures both genuine prospectors and others wanting to make a quick buck from the naive, much like the 'gold rush' ages of old. The latter is sometimes disguised as spectacular marketing efforts, guarantees of assured profits, or even celebrity endorsements. A wise investor would do well to look beyond the luster. Regulatory clearances, ratings from reputable financial analysts, and even peer reviews are all indicative of a platform's legitimacy.

Understanding the nature of digital investments is also critical. Unlike real assets, where actual possession is commonly used to imply ownership, digital assets depend on cryptographic keys, complicated algorithms, and the like. A basic comprehension of these guarantees that an investor's judgments are not based just on hope but on some degree of technical knowledge.

Furthermore, the simplicity with which digital assets may be acquired, sold, or swapped can be both a gift and a curse. This may cause a flurry of buying and selling for the inexperienced, frequently to their cost. The age-old adage of 'not placing all your eggs in one basket' applies here. Diversifying across several digital assets, like one would in a conventional portfolio, may help limit risks.

Finally, the fundamental power of the digital era is found not in its algorithms or platforms but in the extraordinary access to information that it provides. By tapping into this large reservoir - whether via online courses, financial forums, or digital periodicals - an investor may arm themselves with the skills required to not just manage but flourish in this new era of investment.

Embracing the Gig Economy:

While stock markets, real estate, and conventional company operations have long been financial growth pillars, the current era offers new opportunities to supplement one's income. The gig economy, which is defined by short-term contracts or freelance labor rather than permanent positions, exemplifies such a transition.

The emergence of platforms catering to freelancers, from writers and graphic designers to programmers and digital marketers, has transformed our perception of work. Individuals may now earn depending on their abilities, availability, and entrepreneurial spirit rather than being tied to a desk or limited by a 9-to-5 schedule. While this freedom is freeing, it also carries with it a unique set of financial problems and possibilities.

When opposed to typical employment, managing funds as a freelancer or gig worker requires a different strategy. Because of the erratic nature of revenue, budgeting becomes critical. Individuals must prepare for their future without the safety net of employer-sponsored health insurance or retirement benefits. This might include putting a portion of their salary away for medical emergencies, investing in retirement money, or ensuring they are appropriately insured.

On the other hand, the gig economy provides unrivaled prospects for financial advancement. Multiple jobs may be pursued at the same time, abilities can be monetized in previously unimaginable ways, and there is a worldwide market just waiting to be tapped. The digital nomad lifestyle, in which people travel the globe while working remotely, has also grown popular, combining the pleasures of travel with the satisfaction of earning.

Most importantly, the move to the gig economy emphasizes the value of independence. The onus is completely on the individual, whether it's staying on top of industry developments, regularly upskilling to stay relevant, or prudently managing one's resources. And herein is the current financial landscape's difficulty as well as its delight.

The Role of Social Media in Shaping Financial Perspectives

The effect of social media stands out as a distinctively contemporary phenomenon in the history of finance. Platforms such as Twitter, Reddit, and TikTok have emerged as unexpected financial venues, affecting investment choices and even spawning wholly new financial trends.

Consider the peculiar example of meme stocks. Certain equities saw stratospheric gains as a result of comments on social media sites, confounding standard market assessments. While some participants profited handsomely, others suffered significant losses, emphasizing the unpredictable nature of such movements and the hazards involved with herd mentality.

However, the influence of social media is not confined to market abnormalities. Influencers possess enormous influence in affecting financial attitudes due to their large followings. A tweet from a well-known individual might cause Bitcoin values to rise or fall. Millions of people watch video clips that teach complex financial topics, democratizing financial education in previously unimaginable ways.

Platforms like Instagram and Facebook have morphed into thriving markets in the business world. Small companies use their reach to sell their goods, interact with consumers, and even conduct transactions. Crowdfunding campaigns on sites like Kickstarter bring new ideas to reality, owing to the online community's pooled financial support.

However, the influence of social media on banking, like other instruments, is a double-edged sword. Because of the quick diffusion of information, rumors and disinformation may spread like wildfire, resulting in hasty financial judgments. The onus is thus on the person to separate reality from fiction and to examine before acting.

In essence, social media is a representation of collective awareness. Its effect on finance highlights a larger fact about the current financial landscape: it is more linked, driven by public mood, and dynamic than ever before. Navigating this world requires a mix of conventional financial knowledge and a grasp of the digital zeitgeist, a combination that offers success in this interconnected era.

Chapter 4

The Psychology of Money

When discussing money, figures, charts, and measurements often take center stage. However, underneath this mathematical surface comes a fundamental qualitative aspect: money psychology. This component is as essential to comprehending finance as mathematics is to accounting. It influences our actions, motivates our ambitions, and frequently dictates our financial fate.

Money is more than just a means of commerce; it is a strong symbol with different connotations across cultures and people. It signifies security to some and freedom to others. It may represent success, power, or even self-esteem. Money's significance, whether conscious or subconscious, impacts our financial habits, risk tolerance, and life choices.

Saving was historically associated with financial prudence. However, in this day and age of investments and assets, merely stashing money isn't always the best option.

However, psychological vestiges of past ideas continue to exist. Some people still see the stock market as a high-stakes casino, and they avoid it not because of a calculated risk assessment but because of deep-seated concerns and misunderstandings.

Similarly, debt, which is a neutral financial instrument in and of itself, is often associated with negative psychological implications. While imprudent borrowing may be disastrous, judicious debt, such as loans for appreciating assets, can be a cornerstone of wealth creation. Breaking away from the psychological constraints that portray all debt as negative is critical for contemporary financial navigation.

Consumerism, spurred by constant advertising, exploits the emotional aspects of money. The attraction of immediate enjoyment might overwhelm the long-term advantages of financial discipline. Recognizing and resisting these urges requires not just willpower but also an awareness of their psychological underpinnings.

Furthermore, as the digital era ushers in abstract financial notions such as cryptocurrency, the psychological struggle becomes more intense. When digital assets are separated from their physical equivalents, they need not just technical understanding but also a psychological adjustment to their intangibility and instability.

Understanding the psychology of money, on the other hand, isn't only about avoiding traps. It's also about maximizing its good impact. The pleasure of reaching financial milestones, the peace of mind that comes with a solid financial future, or the excitement of a successful investment are all powerful motivators. Financial planning may be transformed from a dull work to an enjoyable trip by using these feelings.

With its many possibilities and problems, the current financial world necessitates a dual strategy. While one hand grasps actual financial tools and strategies, the other must dive into the ethereal domain of our monetary beliefs, anxieties, and ambitions. As the saying goes, "Know thyself." In the realm of contemporary finance, this introspective understanding, paired with exterior wisdom, is the crux of genuine financial mastery.

How emotions influence financial decisions: Fear of loss, greed, FOMO.

Analysis Paralysis and Financial Decision-making

The current age, aided by technological improvements, provides a dizzying choice of possibilities in the domain of personal finance. From the many investment vehicles accessible to the sheer amount of tools available for trading, budgeting, and financial management, the information at our disposal may be a double-edged sword at times. In the past, the idea of 'choice' was restricted, with fewer options for financial endeavors accessible. That terrain has grown significantly since then.

This enormous diversity, although exhilarating, may also lead to "analysis paralysis." increased options, as Barry Schwartz indicates in "The Paradox of Choice," may not always lead to increased pleasure. Instead, they often increase worry and anxiety, especially when it comes to major financial choices. How does one choose the best cryptocurrency from thousands? Which robo-advisor best matches one's financial objectives?

The dread of making the incorrect decision may be debilitating in such situations. Individuals may find themselves studying constantly, second-guessing their actions, or, worse, choosing inaction out of dread of possible regret. This indecision might cause crucial financial choices to be postponed, resulting in squandered opportunities.

Furthermore, the sheer number of information available online means that people are constantly assaulted with the triumphs of others, whether it's a profitable stock selection or a real estate endeavor. While it's natural to seek advice and learn from others' experiences, continual exposure may lead to unnecessary pressure to follow someone else's route rather than construct one's own unique financial journey according to individual circumstances and aspirations.

To traverse this vast digital landscape, it is critical to first define one's financial goals and risk tolerance. Simplifying options, getting expert help when necessary, and accepting that no one solution fits all may lead to more informed and pleasant financial decisions.

The Psychological Aspects of Cryptocurrency Investments

Cryptocurrency growth has been nothing short of spectacular. What began with Bitcoin has now grown into a diversified ecosystem of digital assets. The attractiveness of cryptocurrencies extends beyond the prospect of large profits; it is linked to a vision of decentralized finance and a future less dependent on established financial institutions.

The world of cryptocurrencies is a psychological case study on trust. Traditional investments, such as stocks and bonds, have a history and are linked to physical entities such as businesses or governments. Cryptocurrencies, on the other hand, are intrinsically intangible and run on the blockchain - a decentralized ledger system.

This decentralization indicates that the asset is not governed by a central authority, such as a central bank, in the case of conventional currencies. This appeals to people who are skeptical of established financial institutions and would prefer a system in which their money is not subject to government regulations or inflationary pressures.

This, however, creates a new set of concerns. The cryptocurrency market's volatility, fueled by speculation and sensitive to market emotion, may result in extreme price movements. This volatility, along with reports of digital heists and lost access to cryptocurrency wallets, may elicit strong emotional reactions in investors, ranging from joy during market peaks to outright fear during market falls.

Furthermore, establishing faith in cryptographic codes and digital wallets might be psychologically challenging, particularly for older generations used to actual possessions. In the crypto realm, the fundamental concept of 'value' is being questioned.

Emotional detachment, proper investigation, and risk evaluation are essential in any financial pursuit. Cryptocurrency is a fascinating combination of technology, money, and psychology, with the potential to reshape the global financial landscape.

The Influence of Social Media on Financial Behaviors:

The infiltration of social media into our everyday lives has been transformational. These platforms have evolved into major influences on behavior, notably in the sphere of finance, in addition to connecting people and sharing memories. The combination of finance and social media has disrupted old paradigms of investing and financial decision-making, from tweets affecting stock markets to influencers advocating the next "hot" cryptocurrency.

For investing advice in the 1990s and early 2000s, most people relied on established financial news channels, advisors, or print periodicals. A TikTok video, an Instagram story, or a hot hashtag may now influence market sentiment. For example, the GameStop stock spike, which was mostly driven by Reddit conversations, demonstrated the collective power of retail investors mobilized via social networks. Likewise, the growth of ' meme' cryptocurrencies underscores the power of virality in today's financial scene.

The democratization of financial knowledge via social media, on the other hand, is a double-edged sword. On the one hand, it provides for a more extensive diffusion of information, allowing many people to get access to insights they would not have had before. However, the fast propagation of unconfirmed information, along with the temptation of immediate rewards, may lead to rash judgments based on excitement rather than facts.

The psychological effect of witnessing peers or influencers brag about their financial successes may also contribute to FOMO (Fear of Missing Out). When everyone seems to be rushing to buy a certain stock or cryptocurrency, the temptation to get on board, lest one lose out on possible rewards, may be enormous. This herd mentality, exacerbated by social media's echo chambers, may occasionally overpower reasonable thought.

It takes discretion to navigate this loud world. It is critical to distinguish between reliable sources and hype peddlers. While social media may be a good beginning point for financial study, further in-depth research, interaction with financial specialists, and contemplation on personal financial objectives are all necessary. The contemporary investor, more than ever, must learn to filter through noise in order to discover true signals.

Scarcity vs. Abundance mindsets and their impact on finances.

Breaking the Cycle of Generational Money Beliefs

Our money ideas, although impacted by our own experiences, are strongly established in our upbringing. Observations and interactions with parents, caretakers, and our local neighborhood impact our financial views and habits from a young age. In the 1990s, most financial ideas and knowledge were spread via family talks, some formal schooling, and word of mouth. While these old routes continue to exist, the internet and the explosion of online financial communities have extended perspectives, questioning and modifying inherited money views.

Consider a youngster in the 1990s hearing a parent complain about a constant shortage of money and compare that to a millennial today, who is bombarded with internet tales of financial independence and early retirement. While the former may subconsciously associate money with everlasting scarcity, the latter may develop an abundance mentality, believing in the potential of building riches through educated judgments and proactive steps.

However, the transmission of money views through generations is not necessarily linear or predictable. Many people today, equipped with huge financial resources and capabilities, try intentionally to unlearn harmful financial notions passed down from their families. They work hard to break the cycles of debt, bad financial choices, or the fear-based attitude to money that may have been common in their families while they were growing up.

It is critical to recognize and fight these inherent financial assumptions. Only then can a personal financial path be carved out, using the best of previous wisdom while maximizing the potential of current resources and knowledge. It is a path of recognizing one's financial background, accepting its effect, and then shaping a future that reflects one's own objectives rather than generational baggage.

Recognizing and Overcoming Them

Everyone, regardless of financial skill, is prone to cognitive biases. These are systemic deviations from reason that may have a major impact on our financial judgments and choices. The current financial world, which is rich with information and options, allows for these biases to develop and even be exploited.

In the era of personalized newsfeeds, for example, the 'confirmation bias' is common. If a person feels that a specific stock is a good investment, they may instinctively seek information that supports that opinion while disregarding evidence that contradicts it. In today's world of easy access to trading platforms, the 'overconfidence bias' may be magnified, enabling inexperienced investors to make hasty judgments based on little understanding.

Another bias, 'loss aversion,' has long been a feature of human psychology. People prefer to avoid losses rather than earn equal rewards. With real-time investing updates, the emotional roller-coaster may be powerful, resulting in impulsive judgments during market instability.

Overcoming these prejudices requires a combination of self-awareness and education. Individuals may build ways to avoid common psychological traps by knowing them. This might include establishing explicit investing criteria ahead of time, soliciting many viewpoints, or just recognizing the emotional component of financial choices and instituting precautions against hasty acts.

With a world flooded with data and voices, the task is not just to identify the best financial plan but also to create a mentality capable of navigating the landscape with judgment and balance.

Delinking Personal Value from Financial Status

The cliché "Money can't buy happiness" has been repeated for decades, yet the contemporary world, with its glitter and glamour, often blurs the line between personal and financial worth. With its show of luxury, today's social media-centric society often exaggerates the fallacy that financial worth is directly related to self-esteem. This viewpoint may lead to a perilous pursuit of external validation, with monetary milestones serving as indicators of personal accomplishment.

The original "Rich Dad, Poor Dad" by Robert Kiyosaki stressed the importance of financial knowledge and intelligence, but there's another dimension to this conversation in the twenty-first century. While Kiyosaki argued for the pursuit of assets above liabilities, the current reinterpretation includes an appreciation of the intangible assets and liabilities we carry inside ourselves - our beliefs, self-esteem, and emotional well-being.

In the 1990s, success might have been defined by the possession of physical possessions such as a house, a vehicle, or a substantial bank balance. While these indicators are still important today, there is a growing acknowledgment of holistic well-being, which encompasses mental health, emotional balance, and a sense of purpose. The significance of reflection, happiness, and personal progress may often be overshadowed by the 'hustle culture' preached by many internet influencers.

It's critical to realize that although one's net worth is important, it's just one piece of the puzzle. Individual experiences, relationships, personal development, and communal contributions are all as, if not more, significant. A large money balance without a sense of purpose or true satisfaction might be a hollow success.

People are more than their bank accounts. The genuine definition of wealth is a well-balanced existence in which riches support goals and necessities but do not determine identity or self-worth. Individuals must create their own measurements that reflect their ideals, goals, and realities in a society where definitions of success are always changing. This internal compass will lead them to true satisfaction and success more than any external yardstick.

Unpacking money scripts

Origins, implications, and altering negative scripts.

How Financial Status Influences Personal Perception

Money has held power not just as a real instrument of transaction but also as an intangible gauge of human success and failure for as long as currency has existed. Many people equated monetary riches with personal accomplishment throughout the 1990s, an era marked by growing economies and significant financial market expansion. Fast forward to today's digital age, and the same attitude exists, but with more fervor, as a result of the constant advertising of affluent lives on social media platforms.

The relationship between financial position and personal identity is a complex subject, particularly when considering the psychological implications. A person's relationship with money is often a complex dance of desires, cultural expectations, and inner self-worth. While the core of "Rich Dad, Poor Dad" centered on assets, liabilities, and financial literacy, this new terrain provides a deeper introspection: understanding how one's financial situation affects one's self-perception.

Consider the contemporary entrepreneur, for whom the success or failure of their enterprise becomes a reflection of their self-worth. Or the retiree who assesses the value of his or her life by the amount of money saved. Today's digital platforms often worsen this equation, as 'likes' and ' shares' give instant approval or criticism, sometimes centered in monetary symbols.

However, as we go further into the current financial world, it's critical to remind readers that, although important, financial status is just one part of a multi-dimensional identity. True riches consist of a diverse set of experiences, connections, learnings, and memories. Money, or the lack thereof, should not dominate one's self-perception. Individuals who grasp this concept may create a more balanced, rich, and comprehensive life story.

Navigating the Emotional Rollercoaster of Financial Ups and Downs

Despite its inanimate nature, money has a powerful potential to elicit a broad variety of feelings. Finances often influence emotional states, impacting overall mental well-being, from the exciting high of a windfall to the crushing weight of debt. While Kiyosaki's initial speech focused on the mechanics of wealth creation, today's financial environment, fraught with volatility and uncertainty, necessitates an emphasis on the emotional journey that comes with financial efforts.

The development of stock trading applications, cryptocurrency swings, and the insecurity of the gig economy all add to emotional ups and downs. Someone may feel exhilaration one day while seeing their stock portfolio increase, only to suffer worry the following day while witnessing a market fall. The issue is to maintain emotional stability in the middle of this turbulent financial environment.

Finances and mental health are intricately intertwined. Anxiety, sadness, and even personal relationships may be exacerbated by financial stress. On the other hand, financial security may provide peace of mind, but it is not a definite guarantee of pleasure.

We must stress self-awareness, resilience, and emotional intelligence as we lead readers through the current intricacies of money. Individuals may make better-educated, level-headed financial choices by identifying and understanding the emotional triggers associated with money. Furthermore, people may build coping techniques for the inevitable financial downturns, ensuring that their mental health stays stable regardless of the condition of their bank statement.

An Evolving Solution to Address Money-Related Anxieties

Financial treatments have evolved as a treatment to help people address and overcome their financial worries in a society where financial obligations weigh heavy on the psyche. The 1990s were a time when the emphasis was on understanding assets, obligations, and the fundamentals of financial education. Today, the conversation around money has changed to recognize its deep link with mental health.

Financial therapists combine the domains of emotional well-being with budgetary assistance, which distinguishes them from standard financial consulting jobs. They want to disentangle the complex web of emotions, prior experiences, and financial practices. For example, someone's hesitation to invest may be founded on a prior financial trauma or a deep-seated fear of losing rather than a lack of information.

Money has always been a symbol of power, prosperity, and independence throughout history. However, it is also a major cause of worry and anxiety. The many financial choices that must be made, whether it is for student loans, mortgages, retirement plans, or even day-to-day budgeting, may be intimidating. When you consider the current dynamics of turbulent stock markets, the unpredictability of cryptocurrencies, and the attraction and demands of consumerism, it's easy to see why financial anxiety is on the increase.

Financial treatments provide clients with a safe location to address these worries, as well as tools to decode their money scripts and alter any bad tendencies. Such treatments aim to improve people's whole connection with money rather than just their monetary balance. It is about developing a mentality in which money is seen as a tool for happiness rather than a cause of unhappiness (The

Psychology of Money by Morgan Housel - StudentStore.pk, 2023).

Dive into this domain to get insights on a more comprehensive approach to finances. It combines the rational with the emotional, guaranteeing that as one's financial portfolio develops, so does one's mental serenity. Understanding and pushing for financial therapy may be the key to a healthy and harmonious relationship with one's money in a society that increasingly recognizes the significance of mental health.

Chapter 5

Managing Emotions in Finances

Emotions play an important, if sometimes overlooked, part in the delicate dance of money. Beyond the numbers and analysis, there is a range of emotions, from the euphoria of a good investment to the agony of rising debt. Understanding and regulating these emotions is an important part of contemporary financial literacy.

The financial world is littered with examples of sophisticated investors making unusual mistakes owing to unrestrained emotions. Fear and greed dubbed the "twin dragons of investing," may distort judgment and tempt even the most seasoned experts to abandon their plans. In turbulent markets, for example, fear might cause quick sales, converting paper losses into actual losses. In contrast, the enthusiasm of a bull market may tempt one to overextend, neglecting underlying values.

Emotions impact daily financial choices in addition to investments. The satisfaction of possessing the most recent technology, the convenience of retail therapy, or societal pressures to "keep up with the Joneses" may all undermine financial discipline. These emotional purchases, which are often justified after the fact, may deplete finances and result in unwanted debts.

The solution, however, is not to eradicate feeling, which is both impracticable and inadvisable. Instead, it is about establishing emotional balance. It is critical to recognize when emotions are impacting choices, pause to analyze their validity, and then move with clarity and purpose.

This balance is even more important in today's digital world. With internet buying available at the push of a button and social media continuously displaying glorified lives, emotional triggers are everywhere. Furthermore, the ease with which one may participate in online trading or cryptocurrency speculation raises the likelihood of rash, emotionally charged judgments.

Education is critical in this situation. Knowledge serves as an anchor, offering security and lowering worry. When faced with a financial quandary, reverting to fundamental ideas, such as the foundations of value investing or the significance of an emergency fund, may assist in managing emotional whirlwinds.

However, it is crucial to recognize and appreciate feelings. After all, overall well-being is the ultimate objective of financial pursuits. Money is a tool for achieving desirable life experiences, such as the pleasure of global travel, the fulfillment of charity, or the security of a comfortable retirement.

The present financial world, with its plethora of options and constant stimulation, demands not just cognitive but also emotional intelligence. Emotional management in finance is not about repression; it is about integration. It's about balancing the aspirations of the heart with the knowledge of the head, creating a financial symphony that resonates with both success and happiness.

The significance of setting financial goals.

The Interplay of Feelings and Fiscal Decisions

Despite their apparent simplicity, financial choices are often impacted by a tangle of emotions and prior experiences. Kiyosaki's first work concentrated on realistic talks about assets and obligations. However, as the current financial environment grows more entwined with everyday life as a result of the pervasiveness of technology, emotions play an even larger role.

One may recollect the rush of excitement that comes with a successful stock choice or the pain of regret that comes with a lost investment opportunity. These normal emotions may occasionally lead to rash judgments. For example, elation following a successful transaction may encourage bolder initiatives, but dread from a loss may create excessive reluctance. Unchecked emotions may distort judgment and lead to deviations from sensible financial strategy.

Humans are not always the rational participants that classic economic theories represent, according to psychology and behavioral finance research. Overconfidence, loss aversion, and herd mentality are all factors that regularly influence choices. Understanding these emotional triggers allows you to construct a barrier against impulsive financial conduct.

The goal is to acknowledge and harness emotions rather than repress them, which is impossible. Adopting a meta-cognitive approach, in which one becomes an observer of their emotions rather than a hostage, may lead to better judgments. The financial rollercoaster does not have to reflect one's emotional condition. With awareness, knowledge, and contemplation, it is possible to find a balance in which emotions enhance rather than derail the financial path.

The Emotional Pitfalls in the Age of Instant Gratification

The notion of rapid gratification has thoroughly penetrated financial practices in today's digital era when transactions can be accomplished with a single click, and investments can be followed in real time. The '90s, as described by Kiyosaki's original book, stressed patience, long-term planning, and the art of delayed gratification. In contrast, today's financial world provides quick benefits as well as equally immediate consequences.

This immediacy culture has downsides. The exhilaration of watching real-time stock market movements may be intoxicating, causing people to choose short-term trading over long-term investment. Similarly, the convenience of internet buying, along with targeted marketing efforts, may lead to impulsive spending sprees that deviate from financial objectives.

In our day and age, the emotional dangers include not just impatience but also continual comparison. Social media platforms promote affluent lives, which may lead to feelings of inadequacy and a need to 'keep up.' This can lead to financial choices that favor exterior appearances over true financial well-being.

Navigating this period requires a reset of beliefs and expectations. It's important to remember that the most rewarding financial achievements typically result from patience, discipline, and dedication to one's objectives. While the digital era provides many possibilities, it is critical to seize them without succumbing to the dangers of quick satisfaction. Individuals may develop a solid financial future that is resilient to the transitory attractions of the present by fostering an introspective mentality and long-term vision.

The Hidden Influences of Past Prices and Perceptions

When Robert Kiyosaki stressed the difference between assets and liabilities, the discussion centered on physical structures. However, as the complexity of behavioral finance comes to the fore, there is a need to dive into subconscious biases that influence our monetary decisions. 'Anchoring' is one such subtle but profoundly important bias.

Anchoring refers to the human inclination to base judgments on a single piece of information (the "anchor"). In the financial world, this is sometimes manifested as prior prices or historical benchmarks. An investor, for example, may regard a stock as 'cheap' if its current price is lower than a previously higher price, even though the present price does not fully reflect the stock's underlying worth.

Anchoring has a wide range of effects. A buyer of real estate may overpay because the asking price is lower than the first inflated price they faced. Alternatively, a retiree may be dissatisfied with a truly decent pension contract merely because their expectations were anchored to a greater amount described previously.

This prejudice extends beyond numbers. Emotional anchors based on previous experiences or tales heard may alter perceptions of investment safety, risk profiles, and even return possibilities. For example, someone who has heard stories of large losses in cryptocurrencies may be inclined to regard it as very hazardous, even if they are unfamiliar with its mechanics or possibilities (Rucker, 2023).

Combating the impact of anchoring requires intentional awareness and ongoing education. Modern readers must be trained to identify and overcome their cognitive biases, much as Kiyosaki highlighted the need for financial literacy in comprehending assets and liabilities. Individuals might avoid becoming unnecessarily anchored by prior pricing or impressions by constantly reassessing financial choices and obtaining various opinions. Freeing oneself from these hidden restraints might pave the way for more informed and objective judgments in the fluid world of finance, where flexibility is vital.

Budgeting essentials.

The Conscious Approach to Spending and Saving

In the original "Rich Dad, Poor Dad," Kiyosaki discussed the concept of financial education and how it plays an important part in one's wealth-building path. With today's variety of distractions and quick transactions, there is an increasing need to examine the notion of 'financial mindfulness.'

Financial mindfulness refers to being deliberately present and purposeful in all of our financial decisions. It is necessary to pause for a minute, take a step back, and carefully consider the implications of each purchase, investment, or financial commitment. In an age where contactless payments, one-click purchases, and fast loans are the norm, it's much too simple to make rash choices that may not correspond with one's long-term financial objectives.

Financial mindfulness is about empowering one's choices rather than constraining oneself. It emphasizes the underlying emotions or causes driving a purchase. Was it a legitimate requirement? A passing desire? Or is it an effort to fill a hole or alleviate stress? We may connect our financial habits with our inner values by understanding the 'why' behind our spending, ensuring that our money is spent or saved in a manner that actually resonates with our life's objectives.

The benefits of practicing financial mindfulness are many. It not only promotes better knowledge and management of one's financial habits, but it also fosters a feeling of satisfaction. After all, money is more than just a means to a goal; it is a tool that when utilized wisely, can improve our lives in more ways than one.

The Emotional Roller Coaster of Debt

Debt, in its different manifestations, has long been a source of contention in financial debates. While Kiyosaki's "Rich Dad, Poor Dad" discussed "good" vs. "bad" debt, there is an urgent need to examine the emotional repercussions of owing money in today's environment.

Debt is an emotional burden for many people, not simply a financial necessity. It evokes sentiments of shame, guilt, and worry. Whether it's a school loan, a credit card payment, or a mortgage, the weight of debt might seem overwhelming at times. However, just as our financial tools and techniques for managing and seeing debt have developed, so have our tools and methods for managing and perceiving debt.

Recognizing the emotional component of debt is the first step in regaining control. It's critical to remember that debt isn't a reflection of one's value or talents in and of itself. Rather than being a negative, it is a tool that, when used properly, may be harnessed for development and opportunity.

One of the most significant changes in current financial thought is the acceptance of debt as part of a bigger financial plan. It's about understanding when to take on debt, how to manage it efficiently, and, most critically, how to keep it from negatively impacting one's mental health. We may negotiate the intricacies of contemporary economics with a clearer mind and a more cheerful attitude if we change our view on debt from a cause of worry to a strategic instrument.

Transforming Envy into Inspiration

Envy has a notably unfavorable reputation throughout the entire range of human emotions, especially in the world of wealth. Every triumph, purchase, or expensive excursion in today's digital era is exhibited on social media, providing a fertile environment for comparison. A peek at a peer's financial success may ignite a flame of envy, often leading to hasty financial choices with long-term consequences.

But what if this same passion could be harnessed in a different way? What if jealousy could be used to spur good financial change?

When broken down, envy is basically an expression of our intrinsic drive for advancement and growth. Seeing another person reach a financial milestone, whether it's buying a prized item or taking a dream trip, elicits a reaction that mimics our own. This isn't inherently harmful. When unrestrained jealousy pushes us into financial battlefields without the armor of vision and plan, a conundrum arises.

Rather than influencing spontaneous judgments, jealousy has the ability to serve as a motivator. Here's a look at how that transition occurred:

To begin, it is critical to start on a road of thought and introspection before jealousy becomes action. Introspection should be used to answer the question, "Why has this specific achievement or possession struck a chord?" Is it woven into the fabric of long-term goals, or is it only a passing fancy? Discovering the origins of jealousy provides clarity on its sincerity, assisting in distinguishing true aspirations from ephemeral infatuations.

Moving ahead, if jealousy is shown as a reflection of genuine desires, it may be used as a drive to define clear, sensible financial objectives. Rather than seeing another's accomplishment as a measure of one's own insufficiency, it might be seen as a source of inspiration, a testimony to what is possible. This paradigm change from passive envy to active inspiration encourages healthy rivalry and progress.

Furthermore, the process of expressing and visualizing these objectives provides a road map for people on their own financial journey. It gives a defined path, guaranteeing that every step performed is in line with the eventual goal.

Automation in savings and its advantages.

Balancing Automation with Intuition

The temptation of automation in financial choices has become greater in our quickly expanding digital world. Automated savings, robo-advisors, and algorithm-driven investing platforms all promise ease and "emotion-free" financial decision-making. But there's an underlying dilemma that often rises to the surface: When does automation cut us off from our financial journeys?

Human emotions and instincts have always played an important part in financial choices, from the days of barter to today's complex financial networks. Trust, intuition, fear, and ambition have traditionally served as the compass that guides our financial ships. While automation offers efficiency and uniformity, there is a danger of being disconnected from the monetary process. Without knowing the mechanics of an automated decision, one may be giving algorithms too much power.

Consider the experience of seasoned investors who, after years of interacting with the markets, acquire an intuition—a 'gut feeling'—about specific assets. This intuition is the result of years of expertise, emotional intelligence, and knowledge of market psychology. A robo-advisor can analyze data quicker than any person, but it lacks the depth of human experience and nuanced knowledge that comes from years of hands-on interaction.

Furthermore, the same emotions that automation aims to eradicate from the financial process may be a benefit at times. When contemplating investments in socially responsible enterprises or weighing the ethical consequences of a specific financial decision, empathy, for example, is critical. Similarly, the delight one experiences after reaching a financial milestone is a tremendous motivation, driving people to become more financially knowledgeable and proactive.

That is not to imply that automation is without use. Automated tools may be an important entrance point for inexperienced investors or people who feel overwhelmed by the immensity of the financial world. These tools may help you create good financial habits, such as saving regularly and diversifying your assets.

The Role of Automated Investments in Achieving Freedom

Over time, the notion of financial independence has developed. It frequently meant amassing enough assets or investments to produce a passive income stream, making a 9-to-5 job obsolete in Robert Kiyosaki's age. With the advancement of technology and automation, the paths to this sought freedom have become more diverse.

Automated investing, whether via robo-advisors or automated savings programs, provides a hands-off approach to wealth accumulation. Based on the user's risk profile, these platforms utilize algorithms to spread investments among different assets. The simplicity of this approach is its beauty: put it up, and the system does the rest.

This automated method may hasten one's path to financial freedom. Regular payments to investment accounts leverage the potential of compound interest, sometimes resulting in considerable long-term gain. Furthermore, by eliminating emotional biases, these platforms can maintain a consistent investing approach, which frequently results in more steady returns.

True financial independence, on the other hand, goes beyond simply monetary acquisition. It is about knowing one's money, making educated choices, and feeling confident about one's financial future. While automation handles day-to-day activities, people should continue to educate themselves, understand where their money is going, and assess and adapt their plans on a regular basis as their objectives change.

Automated investments provide a new means of achieving an age-old aim. But, at its core, financial independence will always be a balance between gaining money and developing the knowledge and confidence to manage and enjoy that riches to the maximum extent possible.

Harnessing Emotional Intelligence in Financial Decisions

In a society obsessed with algorithms and automation, the importance of emotional intelligence (EQ) in financial choices is sometimes overlooked. However, as we negotiate an increasingly complex financial world, understanding our emotions and their impact on our actions becomes critical.

In the 1990s, the concept of EQ arose, stressing the capacity to detect, analyze, and control our own emotions while also being sensitive to the emotions of others. While it has usually been associated with interpersonal relationships, its use in the field of personal finance is extensive. A high EQ may serve as a beacon, leading us securely across the turbulent seas of financial decision-making.

Self-awareness is one of the characteristics of emotional intelligence. This entails identifying our emotional triggers, particularly when it comes to money. For example, a person may become aware that they engage in retail therapy when they are worried or nervous. Recognizing this tendency is the first step toward reducing waste and making more careful spending decisions.

Then there's self-regulation, which is another pillar of EQ. We can focus on moderating our reactions after we've discovered our triggers. This might include instituting methods to prevent impulsive purchases, such as waiting 24 hours before purchasing a non-essential item or designating a separate budget for discretionary spending.

Empathy is also important. It influences how we make collaborative financial choices, particularly in families or relationships. Understanding your partner's financial concerns, goals, and beliefs may lead to more collaborative and helpful financial planning.

EQ improves our interpersonal abilities, which are critical when negotiating terms of a contract, obtaining financial guidance, or resolving financial issues. Being able to speak effectively, listen attentively, and resolve problems without becoming unduly emotional might result in better financial results.

Incorporating emotional intelligence (EQ) into our financial lives does not imply ignoring the rational or analytical parts of decision-making. Instead, it's about balancing the two, ensuring that our decisions are inspired by a healthy combination of reason and emotional understanding rather than just fleeting feelings.

Seeking professional assistance: When and why.

Navigating the Emotional Pitfalls of Financial Independence

Emotions may be both our staunchest ally and our most dangerous opponent in the search for financial freedom. Our financial judgments as humans are not always the result of rational conclusions; they are linked with our sentiments, experiences, and intrinsic prejudices.

For many, the road to financial independence is painted with visions of liberation - freedom from employment, freedom from social expectations, and freedom from financial worry. While the goal is tempting, the journey is filled with emotional perils. These emotional pitfalls may often overshadow the freedom sought.

Consider the attraction of keeping up with the Joneses. In our digital era, the Joneses are not just our next-door neighbors but also social media influencers, displaying a life of luxury travel, high-end devices, and gourmet meals. The urge to conform, to enhance one's lifestyle as one's wealth rises, may be intense. This tendency, known as lifestyle inflation, has the potential to undermine even the most carefully prepared financial strategies.

Then there's the decision conundrum. With so many financial options available to us, from stocks and bonds to cryptocurrency, making a decision may be difficult. Analysis paralysis, brought on by the dread of making the "wrong" decision, may result in inactivity. In the realm of investment, inactivity is often more expensive than making a poor decision.

But it's not all doom and gloom. Recognizing and avoiding these emotional hazards is half the fight. Financial education may give the insight required to traverse these emotional minefields. When this information is combined with introspection, it may result in a healthy blending of money and sentiments, where emotions enhance the path without derailing it.

Reframing Wealth: Beyond the Tangibles

For millennia, wealth has been associated with tangible possessions such as real estate, gold, stocks, and the amount in one's bank account. However, as we go further into the complexities of personal finance in the current day, there is a growing realization that genuine wealth is more than simply what is physical.

Time, for example, is a kind of riches. The ability to spend one's time as one wishes, free of financial constraints, might be more precious than any possession. It's the luxury of a leisurely morning coffee, the excitement of impromptu travel, or the peace of a midweek afternoon spent reading.

Health is also a valued sort of wealth. No amount of money can buy the happiness of a healthy body and mind. The quest for financial prosperity often comes at the expense of one's health, whether via stress, sedentary habits, or a lack of time for self-care.

Another pillar of intangible wealth is relationships, which are strengthened by true connections, trust, and mutual respect. Happiness acquired through genuine connections shared moments of delight, and consolation in times of grief often eclipses worldly wealth.

It is critical to achieve a balance while conceptualizing wealth. While monetary riches give protection and provide doors to new possibilities, it is frequently the intangible types of prosperity that create deeper, longer-lasting enjoyment. Recognizing and cherishing various types of riches, while yet seeking financial advancement, may lead to a more comprehensive, rewarding view of prosperity.

Chapter 6

Diversifying Income Streams

The age-old adage, "Don't put all your eggs in one basket," remains vitally pertinent in the ever-changing world of banking. Though not new, the notion of diversifying income sources has taken on new relevance in today's complex financial world.

Historically, many people relied on single, stable employment for financial stability. A profession, which may span decades at a single business, offered a steady income, paving the way for life's milestones such as purchasing a house, raising a family, and retiring comfortably. However, the global economy's tectonic movements, driven by technological advances, have made this paradigm less sustainable and, for many, less desirable.

Welcome to the age of diverse income. Depending on a single source of money today is not only financially dangerous but it also restricts possible growth. In this sense, diversification involves obtaining money from several sources, lessening reliance on any single one.

Several aspects highlight the significance of this method. To begin with, conventional job stability has become scarce. Economic downturns, firm downsizing, and the fast speed of technological progress may quickly make certain occupations obsolete. Having numerous revenue sources functions as a financial buffer, maintaining stability even if one source of income diminishes or disappears.

Second, the digital revolution has created a slew of new possibilities. The Internet has democratized revenue generating, from freelance digital marketing to selling homemade products online or tuition in specialized areas. These aren't only for the technologically savvy millennials. People of all ages are using Internet platforms to monetize their talents and interests.

Furthermore, the emerging gig economy offers flexibility and liberty, enabling people to make money on their own terms. Platforms such as ridesharing applications and freelancing marketplaces have made side hustles more accessible and common.

There's also the area of passive income. Investing in stocks, bonds, or real estate may provide compounded gains over time. The current environment also includes innovations such as peer-to-peer financing and income from digital content that, once established, need little continuous work.

Diversifying your revenue sources, however, is not without its obstacles. It requires time, effort, and, in many cases, an initial financial commitment. Furthermore, managing many projects requires shrewd time management and constant flexibility.

Diversifying revenue sources is no longer only a strategy for the wealthy or the entrepreneur. It's a practical method for securing one's economic future in today's volatile financial environment. Diversification does not imply pursuing every possibility but rather determining which routes correspond with one's talents, hobbies, and financial objectives. This creates a resilient and strong financial tapestry that is ready to withstand storms and grab opportunities in equal measure.

The importance of multiple streams of income revisited.

Harnessing the Gig Economy for Financial Resilience

The phrase 'gig economy' would have been unheard of in 1997. Nonetheless, it signals a historic change in the way people work and earn. The gig economy provides several chances to create revenue on one's own terms, from driving for ridesharing platforms to freelancing on worldwide markets. For many, it is no longer a side business but a major, if not main, source of income.

But what does this entail for the person navigating the 21st-century financial maze? It denotes flexibility and agility. The standard 9-to-5 job, long thought to be the pinnacle of financial security, is now simply one of many ways to make money. While it delivers a consistent salary, the gig economy also gives flexibility, autonomy, and, in many cases, the opportunity for better wages depending on effort and expertise.

Furthermore, participation in the gig economy might provide a safety net. In an unpredictable economic climate, having various freelancing or part-time employment might help protect against unforeseen financial shocks. If one stream runs dry, others may fill in. However, it is critical to approach this with caution and planning. Diversifying within the gig economy, for example, by combining content production with teaching or graphic design, may lessen risks and assure a more consistent revenue flow.

However, this new terrain is not without its obstacles. Gig workers endure wage unpredictability, a lack of conventional benefits, and the need for ongoing skill development. The gig economy, on the other hand, provides a potential route to financial independence and freedom for people willing to accept change, adapt, and learn.

The Revolution of Passive Income in the Digital Age

If the original "Rich Dad, Poor Dad" emphasized the benefits of passive income, the digital era has altered its very essence. In essence, passive income is money produced with little to no active work. Previously, this was often associated with real estate rents or income from investments. While they are still important, the digital sphere has given rise to a slew of new options.

Consider digital items such as eBooks, online courses, or software that can be downloaded. Once made, they may be marketed indefinitely with no requirement for actual manufacture or shipment. Consider affiliate marketing, in which people earn a commission by advertising items or services. This may become a reliable source of revenue if you have a well-established blog or social media presence.

There are other venues, such as YouTube or podcasting, where content producers may make money via adverts, sponsorships, or fan contributions. These channels, although requiring some initial effort in content development, may yield cash long after the task is completed.

A word of caution, though, is in order. The attraction of passive income often obscures the upfront work, patience, and strategy necessary. Not every eBook goes on to become a best-seller, and not every YouTube channel receives millions of views. Approaching digital passive income sources with knowledge, a clear strategy, and a dedication to providing actual value is critical. With these in place, the digital era provides unprecedented opportunities for individuals willing to innovate and strategically spend their time and abilities.

Modern Financial Tools and Their Role in Wealth Building

Personal financial and wealth-building tools were reasonably basic in the late 1990s. The conventions were traditional banking, stock market investments via brokers, and physical assets such as real estate. Today, the plethora of financial instruments accessible would seem almost extraterrestrial to someone from that age.

Online platforms and applications have democratized money in unprecedented ways. A considerable amount of cash is no longer required to begin investing. Platforms allow users to purchase fractional shares, which means they may own a portion of their favorite company for a small fee. The stock market is now accessible to millions of people who previously thought it was just for the wealthy.

Aside from the stock market, there are peer-to-peer lending sites that enable users to play banker by lending money to peers in exchange for interest. This direct arrangement eliminates conventional financial middlemen, which often results in lower interest rates for both the borrower and the lender.

Cryptocurrencies and blockchain technology reflect the financial transformation of our period. Beyond being a speculative asset, cryptocurrencies provide a decentralized means of transacting, investing, and even earning interest or dividends through staking or DeFi systems.

Then there's the emergence of robo-advisors, which are algorithm-driven systems that automate investing depending on a person's risk tolerance and objectives. These advisers have made it easier for people, particularly those who are new to investing, to effectively diversify their portfolios.

However, with the abundance of tools comes the issue of selection. Which platform should I use? Which assets should I invest in? How much risk should I take? While the current financial environment offers opportunity, it also necessitates a greater level of financial understanding. Blindly plunging in, enticed by stories of instant riches, might result in huge losses (Herrick, 2023).

As a result, education is critical. Today's instruments make it possible to achieve financial independence quicker than ever before, but they also introduce new problems and hazards. Navigating this needs a combination of old-school financial knowledge, as promoted by books like "Rich Dad Poor Dad," and current awareness of the instruments at our disposal. This combination of information and technology enables people to accurately and confidently predict their financial futures.

Exploring new-age avenues:

Understanding the Dynamics of Passive Income in the Digital Era

According to Kiyosaki, passive income was formerly associated with rental income, dividends, and maybe royalties from intellectual property. However, with the emergence of the digital era, the canvas of passive income sources has increased tremendously. It's critical to understand how these possibilities have developed in both quantity and kind.

The Internet of today is brimming with options that challenge the old notion of "working for money." Digital items, for example, need just one creation and may be sold eternally with no extra expenditures. Consider a well-crafted online course, eBook, or piece of software. These products, once built, may generate money with little to no continuing work as long as they stay relevant to their intended demographic.

Affiliate marketing, yet another digital era miracle, enables individuals to earn a commission by advertising the goods of others (or companies). The benefit of this strategy is that no time or effort is required to generate a product or service. They simply capitalize on pre-existing demand, using the tools and channels available today to reach out to prospective clients.

Subscription models, particularly in content production platforms like Patreon or specialized community forums, enable producers to collect recurring compensation from their subscribers or 'patrons.' This strategy recognizes and rewards audience loyalty, ensuring artists have a steady cash source.

However, with all of these possibilities comes the necessity for discretion. Not every source of passive income is a gold mine. To get started, strategic thought, market research, and occasionally an initial investment are required. Furthermore, the ' set it and forget it' mentality may not always be applicable. Digital items may need upgrades, affiliate partnerships may shift, and subscription material may need to be refreshed on a regular basis.

As a result, although the digital domain provides several passive income opportunities, it also necessitates a proactive attitude. As usual, continuous learning is at the heart of success. Individuals may better position themselves to capitalize on these new-age possibilities by understanding their dynamics, ensuring they don't simply work for money but also make their money work for them.

Real Estate in the Digital World:

Real estate has long been a key component of wealth-creation methods. Kiyosaki's attention to it demonstrates its enduring popularity. However, the way we deal with real estate as an investment vehicle has undergone a digital shift.

Crowdfunding platforms have emerged as a novel means of democratizing access to real estate assets. Investing in successful real estate transactions used to require substantial funds, making it an exclusive playground for the rich. Today, crowdfunding enables several investors to combine their funds and get access to high-value assets or projects.

Furthermore, the advent of virtual worlds is putting the idea of ' space' into question. Virtual real estate, or places inside online digital ecosystems, has gained popularity and is being sold for large quantities of money. While this may seem to be a science fiction premise, early adopters are betting big on its possibilities.

However, like with any investment, knowing the market is critical. While crowdfunding has made it easier to get started, it has also added the difficulty of remote administration and due diligence. Because virtual real estate is still in its infancy, it comes with its own set of dangers and uncertainties.

What is constant is the need for study, due diligence, and a well-thought-out approach. While technologies and platforms improve, the fundamental knowledge of informed investment is as important as it has always been. As the real estate industry expands into digital areas, grasping its complexities becomes critical for the contemporary investor.

From Spare Time to Prime Time

A recurring subject in "Rich Dad, Poor Dad" is the concept of entrepreneurial pursuits or side companies as paths to financial independence. In the 1990s, they were often portrayed as side jobs such as lawn maintenance, teaching, or small-scale retailing. However, the digital revolution has altered the side hustle notion, increasing its potential and vitality.

Side hustles in the past often needed physical presence, a tangible product or service, and were geographically constrained. Fast forward to now, and the Internet has removed many of these constraints. A great graphic designer in Buenos Aires can now service a customer in Tokyo, a writer in Cairo can now write pieces for a magazine in Toronto, and an app developer in Mumbai may now launch apps for a worldwide audience. That is the allure of the digital economy.

Online markets, freelancing platforms, and direct-to-consumer technologies have vastly enlarged the possibilities for aspiring entrepreneurs. They provide a wealth of chances to monetize previously regarded hobbies, abilities, or interests. Photography, for example, has developed from a leisurely art form to a profitable business, with platforms enabling photographers to sell their catches globally.

The content production tsunami has been another paradigm shift in the side hustle scene. Platforms such as YouTube, TikTok, and podcasts have made it possible for producers to commercialize their work, increasing both fame and money. These networks have given birth to influencers and artists who often earn far more than traditional salaries.

However, the idea of a side hustle is changing as a result of this change. For many, what begins as a side hustle frequently expands to become their principal source of income, demonstrating the potential of new digital alternatives.

However, it is critical to traverse this terrain with care and knowledge. Not every side hustle will be a success. Market saturation, platform algorithms, and the necessity for ongoing upskilling may all be obstacles. Furthermore, the digital world is ever-changing. What is popular now may be out of date tomorrow. As a result, ongoing learning, market research, and adaptation are critical.

While the principle of the side hustle remains consistent with Kiyosaki's lessons, the digital era has revolutionized its implementation and potential. Embracing this new paradigm requires a combination of old-school work ethic and new-age digital competence. As possibilities expand, so does the need for smart side hustle ecosystem navigation.

Pros and cons of these new streams in today's world.

A Deep Dive into E-Commerce

The digital revolution has reshaped the contours of trade. Setting up a retail shop in the days of "Rich Dad, Poor Dad" would normally include procuring a physical storefront, dealing with inventory, and participating in on-the-ground marketing. Fast forward to the present, and the business model has shifted dramatically, with e-commerce taking center stage.

E-commerce, often known as electronic commerce, is the practice of purchasing and selling products or services through the Internet. It has leveled the playing field, allowing anybody with an idea and an internet connection to start a business. Platforms such as Shopify, WooCommerce, and Etsy have made it simpler than ever for aspiring entrepreneurs to launch their businesses. Even massive marketplaces such as Amazon enable independent vendors to access a large audience through their platforms.

This shift has several benefits. For starters, it removes geographical limitations, allowing you to serve a worldwide customer. Because there are no expenditures associated with physical storefronts, the overheads are often lower than in conventional retail. It's also adaptable; an e-commerce shop can be operated from anywhere, whether it is a beach in Bali or a café in Paris.

However, the world of e-commerce is not without its difficulties. With minimal entrance hurdles, competition is fierce. It's easy to get disoriented in a sea of various internet retailers. While getting started is simple, growing needs smart digital marketing, SEO knowledge, and client retention methods. There is also the issue of logistics and ensuring that things get to clients in perfect shape and on schedule.

Furthermore, the nature of Internet commerce necessitates vigilance against cybersecurity risks, data breaches, and fraudulent transactions. Another challenge is establishing trust in a virtual world where clients cannot touch or feel things before buying.

However, with these difficulties comes enormous potential. The worldwide e-commerce business is expanding rapidly and shows no signs of stopping. Understanding this domain, with its intricacies and promise, is essential for the contemporary entrepreneur.

Navigating Short-Term Engagements and Freelance Work

Another significant change since the days of "Rich Dad, Poor Dad" is the growth of the gig economy. Historically connected with musicians or performers for a single engagement, the word "gig" has now been co-opted to designate a broad range of short-time, temporary occupations in a variety of sectors.

This model has come to life thanks to the digital era. Upwork, Fiverr, and TaskRabbit have emerged to link freelancers with customers. Ridesharing applications such as Uber and Lyft have made it possible for consumers to make money by utilizing assets they already own, such as their automobiles.

Being a member of the gig economy provides flexibility that regular work does not. Individuals may select tasks that match their abilities and interests, work from anywhere, and typically set their own schedules. This independence may lead to a better work-life balance and the capacity to explore numerous revenue sources at the same time.

However, the gig economy is not without its drawbacks. The lack of employment stability, perks such as health insurance, and obvious professional advancement might be intimidating. Income may be volatile, and seasons of drought without projects might be difficult. Self-discipline is also required; with freedom comes the duty of self-management, ensuring deadlines are fulfilled and quality is maintained.

Furthermore, although platforms have made it simpler to obtain employment, commissions are sometimes charged, lowering the worker's take-home compensation. There's also the issue of differentiation: how to stand out in a marketplace crowded with others providing comparable services.

Despite these obstacles, the attractiveness of the gig economy is clear, particularly for people who value autonomy and diversity in their working life. Understanding how to position oneself, establish a strong personal brand, and continually give value may lead to success in an ever-changing world.

Harnessing the Power of Passive Income in the Digital Age

The appeal of passive income endures. Since the days of barter systems, many people have wished for money to work for them rather than for them to work for it. In "Rich Dad Poor Dad," Robert Kiyosaki introduced readers to the notion of passive income and emphasized its importance in reaching financial independence. While the value of passive income remains unchanged in the twenty-first century, the methods for obtaining it have changed drastically.

The digital era provides people with new and diverse chances to create and profit from passive income sources. One of the most common methods is to use digital materials.

Websites, for example, may be monetized in a variety of ways. From affiliate marketing, in which one promotes items and receives a fee on each sale made through a referral link, to hosting advertisements, in which cash is created every time a visitor interacts with an advertisement. Creating a successful blog or specialized website might lead to a steady income. What's more, the finest part? Once set up and adjusted, these assets may generate revenue with little to no involvement.

Another option is to create digital items. This may include e-books, online courses, stock pictures, and software applications. Unlike physical goods, digital goods may be developed once and sold eternally without incurring further expenditures for each unit. Platforms like Udemy, Shutterstock, and Gumroad make it simpler than ever to distribute and sell such things to a worldwide audience.

Investments have adapted to the digital sphere as well. Individuals may now distribute assets in diverse portfolios according to their risk tolerance thanks to the advent of robo-advisors and online investing platforms. Platforms make sophisticated, data-driven choices that ensure funds grow over time, all while the person reaps the rewards without the day-to-day headaches of active management.

However, the road to profitable passive income is not without its difficulties. Setting up sustainable sources often needs an initial time effort, monetary investment, and ongoing learning. The digital world is fluid, with algorithms, trends, and audience preferences changing all the time. It is critical to be current and adaptable.

Furthermore, with so much information accessible online, distinguishing real prospects from passing fads or blatant frauds is critical. A thorough study, soliciting testimonies, and frequently following one's intuition may be beneficial.

Chapter 7

Modern Real Estate Insights

Real estate, long regarded as a reliable investment vehicle and a method of accumulating long-term wealth, is central to the financial strategy. However, the global economy's transformation and the introduction of technology have altered its dynamics, forcing a new viewpoint on the industry.

Real estate data is now more accessible than ever before in the digital era. Gone are the days when prospective buyers or investors relied only on real estate agents for property information. Today, a plethora of platforms provide detailed property listings, comparative market evaluations, and even virtual tours, allowing educated selections to be made without ever stepping foot on the property.

Short-term rentals have developed as a significant trend, with sites such as Airbnb transforming the conventional accommodation business. Properties are no longer only long-term investments or residences; they are prospective revenue streams that may be leased to global visitors on a short-term basis. This move not only provides property owners with freedom and additional money, but it also requires skilled management to ensure regular occupancy and maintenance.

Real estate crowdfunding has democratized property investing. Previously, substantial cash was required to join this sector. Individuals may now invest lesser sums in varied real estate projects via collective investment platforms, substantially decreasing individual risk and opening the door to profitable possibilities traditionally reserved for the wealthy.

Another aspect of the current real estate scene is tech-augmented property management. Technology simplifies and expands real estate operations, from smart home interfaces that increase property value to management software that assists landlords in managing rent, maintenance, and tenant contact.

However, the digital era carries with it new obstacles. Potential investors may get paralyzed by the amount of information accessible online. Furthermore, the worldwide accessibility of property listings implies increased competition, demanding efforts to differentiate homes in crowded areas.

The growth of urbanization, along with environmental concerns, has pushed sustainability to the forefront of contemporary real estate. Energy-efficient buildings, green construction materials, and sustainable design are more than just buzzwords; they have an impact on purchasing choices and property prices.

The real estate market is more volatile than ever. While the fundamental idea remains true — real estate is a physical asset with intrinsic value — strategies for realizing its full potential have developed. Embracing these current insights is critical for anybody trying to successfully navigate the property market. After all, knowing and responding to current trends isn't just about being relevant; it's also about anticipating and embracing future possibilities.

Traditional real estate vs. modern trends.

The Rise and Relevance of Short-Term Rentals in Modern Real Estate

In the past, real estate was associated with long-term investments in which property was purchased and then either sold for a profit years later or leased out on a yearly basis.

However, with the introduction of platforms like Airbnb, Vrbo, and other similar businesses, the entire fabric of home renting has changed. Short-term rentals, mainly for vacations or short stays, have grown in popularity as a viable revenue stream for property owners and investors.

These short-term leases have several benefits. For starters, they let property owners benefit during peak seasons, such as festivals or holidays, by charging premium rates that often outperform those earned by long-term renters. Furthermore, it provides flexibility; the owner may choose when the property is offered for rent and when it is not. This is especially advantageous if the owner intends to utilize the property for personal purposes just on occasion.

Second, the digital platforms that serve this business are developed for usability and worldwide reach. This guarantees that properties advertised get maximum exposure, resulting in increased occupancy rates. The built-in review systems increase confidence among prospective tenants, enabling property owners with strong ratings to raise their asking rates even more.

This new approach, however, is not without its difficulties. Regulatory obstacles, such as local or country-specific rental legislation, may have an influence on the viability and profitability of short-term rentals. A larger focus is also placed on property management; frequent visitor rotations need continuous upkeep, cleaning, and maybe coping with more wear and tear than typical rentals.

Democratizing Property Investments

The departure from the conventional wisdom that property investing requires substantial cash is a key movement in contemporary real estate. Pooling resources to invest in real estate has become a possibility thanks to crowdfunding platforms built particularly for this purpose. This implies that instead of a single person or corporation owning a property, numerous investors may band together and contribute a portion of the purchase price.

Crowdfunding in real estate enables people to invest in properties that they otherwise would not be able to afford. It provides a diversified approach to real estate investing, allowing an investor to build a portfolio of partial stakes in numerous properties, dispersing risk.

Furthermore, these platforms often have professional management. Most real estate crowdfunding platforms provide professionally managed properties, removing the need for investors to get involved in the day-to-day issues of property management.

Real estate crowdfunding, like other investments, is not without risk. Market downturns, property depreciation, or bad management may all have an influence on returns. Furthermore, liquidity might be an issue. Unlike stocks or bonds, which can be sold immediately, getting out of a crowdfunded property investment may take more time.

The modern world has transformed real estate, a cornerstone of investment plans, with technology breakthroughs and new business structures. While the core of property as an asset stays constant, the methods for acquiring, managing, and profiting from it vary. Embracing these developments while knowing the attendant dangers might open up new opportunities for investors to enhance their wealth.

Enhancing Efficiency and Experience

With the advent of technological breakthroughs, property management, which was formerly viewed as a hands-on, sometimes time-consuming task, has experienced a revolutionary change. Property owners and managers no longer have to depend only on manual techniques to address tenant questions, maintenance concerns, or rent collections. A convergence of software solutions and digital technologies has transformed property management into a simplified, efficient, and user-friendly process for both landlords and renters.

The suite of property management software available on the market is at the heart of this change. These solutions, created with the customer in mind, provide a comprehensive dashboard that combines all aspects of property administration. These solutions significantly minimize the administrative load on property managers, from marketing properties and screening possible renters to automating rent collection and resolving maintenance issues. A significant component is automation, which guarantees that operations such as lease renewals, rent reminders, and even some parts of property upkeep (such as regular inspections) run smoothly and without human interaction.

Beyond the fundamentals, the use of AI and machine learning provides further benefits. Predictive analytics, for example, may estimate maintenance requirements based on past data and give insights about possible openings. This kind of predictive data enables property managers to plan more effectively, resulting in increased occupancy rates and more timely property maintenance.

The digital revolution in property management offers a better experience for tenants. Tenants may use modern methods to discover apartments with virtual tours, sign leases digitally, and pay rent online. Furthermore, the ability to register maintenance requests digitally and watch their progress in real time offers a level of openness and convenience that was previously lacking.

However, like with any digital changes, there are problems. Property managers must exercise caution while selecting the appropriate platforms, maintaining data security, and remaining current with the fast speed of technology changes. Relying heavily on technology may sometimes result in outages or errors that disrupt business. Furthermore, although technology may improve many elements of property management, the human touch is unrivaled. Automated systems cannot completely replace nurturing tenant relationships, recognizing particular requirements, and providing a human touch in interactions.

The convergence of technology and property management represents a larger trend in the contemporary world: the use of digital technologies to improve old procedures (Emerging Trends in Real Estate, 2023). While technology offers tremendous tools for increasing efficiency and enjoyment, the combination of technology and the irreplaceable subtleties of human connection will decide the success of contemporary property management.

Exploring short-term rentals.

A New Age Real Estate Strategy

Property crowdfunding, while being a relatively new idea, has quickly established itself as a critical strategy in the real estate business. This democratized approach to real estate investing enables anyone to spend lesser sums on properties, thus removing the significant entry hurdles that conventional real estate investments pose.

Historically, entering the real estate market required large funds, particularly for homes in exceptional locations or with great upside potential. With the emergence of property crowdfunding sites, however, prospective investors may now engage in profitable real estate possibilities with a little investment. One may possess a fractional interest in properties by combining money with other investors and receiving profits proportionate to their investment.

Furthermore, the advantages go beyond just having access to finance. Property crowdfunding sites often include teams of professionals who thoroughly examine properties before advertising them. This guarantees that investors, particularly those who are new to real estate, are provided with prospects that have been well-researched. This reduces the risks of bad property selection and, in many circumstances, eliminates the need for investors to get involved in the delicate aspects of property management.

However, property crowdfunding, like any other investment technique, is not without its difficulties. While it provides diversity, the structure of pooled investments limits individual investors' authority over property selections. Furthermore, liquidity may be an issue. Unlike stocks, which can be easily sold on the open market, withdrawing one's investment from a crowdfunded property may take more time, particularly if the site does not support such exchanges.

Property crowdfunding appears as a captivating thread in the broad fabric of contemporary real estate investment techniques. It reflects a larger movement in today's financial environment toward more accessibility and democratization. Understanding the complexities of this approach, comparing its benefits against its drawbacks, and finding its placement within a bigger investing portfolio will be critical for the contemporary reader.

Virtual Tours and Augmented Reality

The digital revolution has left no stone untouched, and real estate is no exception. This business has always been driven by physical contacts - site visits, property inspections, and face-to-face discussions. The use of virtual tours and augmented reality (AR) in property listings has been one of the most notable breakthroughs.

Virtual tours provide prospective buyers and tenants with a digital tour of homes. These tours use panoramic photos and movies to simulate the sense of being physically present at the destination. This not only saves time but also broadens the potential market for a home since interested individuals from far-flung places may now 'visit' without having to go.

This is taken a step further with augmented reality. Using a smartphone or AR glasses, prospective buyers may digitally arrange furniture inside a house or even remodel its interiors. This immersive experience enables people to imagine themselves living in the space and adapting it to their tastes and requirements before making a commitment.

Such technical improvements provide significant advantages. They boost property selection efficiency, save time and money on actual visits, and may greatly extend the pool of possible buyers or tenants. Furthermore, in uncertain times when actual visits may be limited, such as during a pandemic, virtual connections might be vital.

However, the tactile experience of a real visit cannot be totally replaced by the immersive nature of technology.

Certain characteristics, such as a neighborhood's vibe or tiny features of a house, maybe best appraised in person. As real estate agents incorporate these technologies, the success of contemporary real estate operations will be defined by finding a balance between technological convenience and the irreplaceable qualities of human relationships.

The Integration of Smart Homes and its Impact on Property Value

The notion of a house has been redefined and stretched beyond bricks and mortar in the middle of the technology revolution. Today's houses, dubbed "smart homes," are intertwined with technology that improves the living experience by adding layers of convenience, safety, and energy efficiency.

The phrase ' phrase smart home' conjures up ideas of voice-activated assistants that can play your favorite music or generate a mood with adjustable lighting. However, the breadth is far greater in actuality. Smart homes integrate technology into practically every aspect of domestic life, from security systems that can be watched and controlled remotely to thermostats that learn your temperature preferences and adapt appropriately. There are refrigerators that warn you when you're short on basics, blinds that adapt according to the time of day, and even gardens that are cared for by automated systems to ensure ideal growing conditions.

These improvements have a wide-ranging influence on property value. On the one hand, with its abundance of technology connections, a smart house is likely to appeal to a contemporary generation that values both luxury and ease. When such a home goes on the market, this might result in a higher asking price. Furthermore, many of these smart technologies, particularly those relating to energy efficiency, may result in significant savings over time, making them appealing investments for long-term homeowners.

The fast progress of technology, on the other hand, provides a distinct difficulty. What is deemed cutting-edge now may become outdated in a matter of years. Potential purchasers may be leery of spending substantially in a house with integrated technology that may become obsolete in the near future. Furthermore, as we progressively integrate technology into our lives, issues regarding data privacy and cybersecurity grow more prominent. With its plethora of linked gadgets, a smart home might potentially be a target for cyberattacks or data breaches.

Understanding the dynamics of smart homes is critical for real estate agents and investors. While they are undeniably the future of housing, their influence on property worth and marketability is a complex subject. One may make educated judgments about investing in smart homes by examining elements such as the lifetime and upgrade possibilities of integrated technology, its value vs. novelty, and the security measures in place.

Introduction to real estate crowdfunding.

The Convergence of Technology and Traditional Real Estate Investing

As the digital age reshapes numerous sectors, real estate, which was formerly assumed to be largely unaffected by technological innovation, is no exception. Traditional real estate investing, defined by direct ownership of physical assets, was often reserved for people with large sums of money. However, as electronic platforms proliferate, this barrier is gradually melting, making property investing more accessible to the common person.

At its essence, crowdfunding is a collaborative effort of individuals pooling their money to support projects initiated by other people or organizations. This methodology, when applied to real estate, has the potential to democratize the investing process. Real estate crowdfunding platforms have arisen as a conduit for prospective investors to connect with property developers or owners in need of financing. Unlike traditional real estate enterprises, where large amounts are sometimes required, crowdfunding platforms allow for modest donations, allowing more individuals to enter the property market.

This move has several advantages. For starters, it spreads risk. An investor may spread their wealth among many projects rather than investing a significant amount into a single property. Furthermore, these platforms often feature a curated selection of properties, enabling due diligence and research to assist investors in making educated judgments.

However, every cloud has a silver lining. While the digital aspect of real estate crowdfunding increases accessibility, it also distances investors from the materiality of their investments. There is a significant difference between visiting a house in person and depending on digital data and photographs. Furthermore, although diversity distributes risk, it may dilute potential profits.

Redefining Property Ownership

The notion of fractional ownership is another intriguing progression in contemporary real estate. While timeshares have been around for a long time, the concept has undergone a digital metamorphosis, resulting in more transparent and adaptable models that appeal to current investing appetites.

As the name implies, fractional ownership permits numerous investors to hold 'fractions' or shares of a property. This system, which in certain cases is augmented by blockchain technology, allows transparent recording of ownership stakes and streamlines the distribution of rental revenue or sale profits based on individual shares.

This concept is particularly suitable for high-value homes in desirable areas that are out of reach for individual investors. By pooling resources, investors may get access to luxury real estate markets, benefiting from both the property's physical advantages and the possibility for financial gains.

However, there are certain factors to consider, as with any investing strategy. Even while technology has reduced the number of ownership conflicts, they might still occur. Furthermore, selling a share in such assets may be less liquid than typical real estate transactions.

As the worlds of technology and real estate continue to mix, new investment opportunities emerge. While these contemporary approaches provide opportunities for many, they also provide their own set of obstacles. As usual, prospective investors should approach with zeal and prudence, equipped with information and a thorough awareness of their financial situation.

Harnessing the Power of PropTech in Real Estate Decision Making

The current real estate sector is experiencing a profound upheaval, fueled by technical breakthroughs known as 'PropTech' or Property Technology. These technologies vary from basic listing platforms to complex artificial intelligence-driven appraisal tools, each of which is transforming the way investors and consumers see real estate.

Traditionally, the hunt for a home might begin with a local newspaper's classified section or a talk with a reputable real estate agent. Virtual tours, neighborhood data, and even augmented reality experiences are now available via Internet platforms, which have eased the process. Potential homeowners or investors may virtually walk around a variety of properties from the comfort of their own homes, removing geographical barriers to decision-making.

Furthermore, the analytical capability that technology brings to the table is unrivaled. Big data analytics technologies sift through massive databases, identifying patterns and insights that may be used to forecast market trends. These technologies, for example, might reveal possible real estate hotspots by evaluating variations in demographic data, traffic patterns, and local company development, providing investors with a competitive advantage. Similarly, by taking into account a larger variety of characteristics than conventional approaches, AI-driven valuation algorithms may produce more accurate property evaluations.

This technology-driven approach also provides more openness. For example, blockchain technology is being tested in several regions of the globe to construct immutable land records. These ledgers have the potential to greatly minimize property disputes, assure correct ownership, and even expedite the notoriously time-consuming property selling process.

Digital platforms also make it easier to develop communities. Even before making a purchasing decision, prospective buyers may interact with current community members to better understand local dynamics. Platforms that integrate smart home technology may provide remote property management solutions for rental homes, ranging from keyless entry to energy usage analytics.

This digital transformation, however, is not without its difficulties. With the expansion of internet platforms, there is a serious danger of information overload. Sifting through a plethora of listings, ratings, and data points may lead to choice paralysis. Furthermore, the human touch and individualized assistance from a seasoned real estate agent may be overpowered by technology at times, possibly losing out on subtle insights gained from years of on-the-ground experience.

Furthermore, like with other digital instruments, security and privacy are top priorities. It is critical to ensure that platforms adhere to strict data protection rules, particularly when sensitive financial data is involved.

The impact of technology on property management and real estate investing.

Virtual Realty and Real-Time Property Valuations

In a society that has steadily embraced the virtual realm, real estate, which has historically been based on actual assets, has had to adapt. Physical site inspections and manual analyses are no longer sufficient for today's investors. The digital sphere has offered up new channels for property market investigation, validation, and transaction, fundamentally changing the approach to real estate.

Property viewings have undergone a fundamental change as a result of virtual tours. The days of scheduling multiple visits to different properties and spending hours commuting are long gone. With 360-degree video technology and virtual reality, a person can now immerse themselves in a house, getting a sense of the area, layout, and even the views without leaving their home. This not only saves time but also allows for a wider search radius, which is extremely useful for foreign or out-of-state investors.

Real-time property values enabled by Artificial Intelligence have further altered the game. AI systems give immediate property evaluations by using massive volumes of data ranging from recent sale prices in the area to the quality of nearby schools. These digital valuations are more than just numbers; they are supported by extensive data analytics that consider a broader range of influencing factors than a human could in a short period of time.

However, although technology provides convenience and speed, it cannot replace the nuanced knowledge and local market experience that seasoned real estate agents provide. Human judgment refines and contextualizes the information provided by digital instruments. For example, an AI may highlight a home as a good deal based on statistics, but a local realtor may be aware of a dump planned nearby, which may affect future property prices.

Furthermore, the dependence on technology needs strong cybersecurity safeguards. Property deals involve large quantities of money, and any misstep might have serious effects. While leveraging technology, investors and property managers should be aware of possible vulnerabilities and protect the security of their digital platforms and transactions.

Real estate technology provides a wide range of opportunities and difficulties. It has the ability to improve the efficiency of operations, the accuracy of choices, and the smoothness of transactions. However, like with any tool, its effectiveness is determined by how it is utilized. In the fast-paced world of real estate, finding the appropriate blend of technology and personal touch is critical to success.

The Rise of Smart Homes and Sustainable Living

With the advancement of technology, contemporary renters' expectations and needs have undergone significant change. The modern renter is searching for residences that fit with their tech-savvy, ecologically sensitive lives rather than merely basic utilities.

Smart homes, which include sophisticated technology such as thermostat controls, voice-activated utilities, and security cameras, are becoming more popular. Such features not only give convenience but also result in long-term cost savings. Intelligent heating systems, for example, may alter room temperatures depending on occupancy, preventing energy from being spent heating an empty room.

Furthermore, as the globe becomes increasingly ecologically concerned, sustainable living has risen to the top of tenant expectations. Green technology, such as solar panels and rainwater collection systems, provide properties a particular advantage. Furthermore, designs that feature green areas for urban farming or that use natural light to ensure energy efficiency appeal to contemporary tenants' ambitions for a sustainable lifestyle.

But it's not only about the property's physical features. Renters nowadays place a premium on community and connection. Shared areas, such as common lounges or offices, appeal to the feeling of community. Furthermore, as the gig economy and remote work grow in popularity, homes with specialized co-working areas or high-speed internet access will have an advantage.

However, while property managers and investors adjust to these changing needs, they must also exercise caution. Integrating smart technology increases the number of possible points of digital access, making cybersecurity critical. Likewise, although sustainable technology provides long-term advantages, the initial expenditure might be substantial. It's critical to assess these expenditures against possible rewards, taking into account both rental fees and long-term energy savings.

How Modern Tools Are Reshaping Investment Strategies

In an era when technology pervades practically every aspect of our lives, real estate is no exception. PropTech, which refers to any real estate-related technology, is fast altering conventional investing techniques. This adoption, fueled by the internet's pervasiveness and the expanding expectations of a digitally literate population, is paving new paths for investors to investigate, assess, and profit from property assets.

Previously, real estate investing was often distinguished by local knowledge, instinct-driven judgments, and, on occasion, a significant documentation trail. Fast forward to the present, and we observe that data analytics systems are providing previously inconceivable insights to investors. An investor may get complete facts about a property's history, understand local property price variations, and even receive predictive analytics about probable future appreciation based on a variety of criteria with just a few clicks. This real-time data access enables investors to make better-educated choices, maximizing profits and avoiding risks.

Beyond data, digital platforms are accelerating transactional efficiency like never before. Geographical distance and other traditional obstacles are becoming outdated. Virtual deal rooms provide real-time document exchange and collaboration, making cross-border investments easier. While blockchain technology is still in its early stages in real estate, it has the potential to make property transactions more transparent, safe, and efficient by eliminating the need for middlemen and speeding up the process.

Augmented reality (AR) is another transformational weapon in the armory of contemporary real estate investors. While virtual tours are becoming more common, augmented reality takes it a step further (McCormick, 2023). Possible investors or purchasers may 'put' virtual furniture in a home or see possible changes to a room to get a sense of what might be. This immersive experience may play a significant role in decision-making.

However, with every benefit comes a catch. Because of the substantial dependence on technology, a thorough comprehension of these tools is also required. Misinterpretation of data or being persuaded only by analytics without taking into account on-the-ground reality might result in expensive miscalculations. Furthermore, although technology helps to speed up operations, the importance of personal connections and networking in the real estate industry remains unrivaled. A knowledgeable local realtor may possess intangible insights that a digital platform may miss.

Chapter 8

Continuous Learning in Finance

Change is the one constant in the ever-changing financial scene. The complicated network of money management is always in motion, from the invention of new financial instruments to alterations in global economic paradigms. This unwavering transition highlights the critical need for constant learning in finance.

The underlying foundations of finance were apparently constant in the age described by Robert Kiyosaki and, once grasped, needed little adjustment. Fast forward to now, and the situation has radically changed. Because of the quick pace of innovation and globalization, financial concepts, strategies, and best practices move through rapid revisions.

The digital economy, a major force in our era, is a monument to the financial sector's capriciousness. With the rise of cryptocurrencies, for example, what was once a niche speculative asset has grown into a full-fledged financial instrument, necessitating a new set of skills and expertise to fully realize its potential. Similarly, although fintech solutions are intended to simplify, consumers must be familiar with its mechanisms in order to reap maximum advantages.

With such instability, resting on one's laurels or relying on old information is a definite way to become obsolete. Continuous learning is, therefore, no longer a luxury; it is a need. Those who are willing to devote time to regular education are in a better position to exploit rising possibilities and avoid mistakes.

Furthermore, constant learning is about improving one's knowledge of financial habits and global market movements, not only adjusting to new technologies or assets. As geopolitical events, environmental issues, and technology breakthroughs alter economies, it is critical to have a deep understanding of these variables.

The contemporary investor, entrepreneur, or financial enthusiast must acquire a student's perspective. This entails actively finding resources — whether they be seminars, online courses, books, or mentorships — to keep up with the newest in finance. They build resilience in this way, ensuring that they are not caught off guard by unexpected financial changes.

As we go through this dynamic financial age, the knowledge of the past, although useful, must be supplemented by modern ideas. The potential of constant learning is unparalleled, working as a compass to steer one through the turbulent waters of contemporary finance. It is, without question, the most formidable weapon in one's financial armory, assuring relevance, flexibility, and long-term success in a fast-paced environment.

The necessity of staying updated in a fast-evolving financial world.

Adapting to New Financial Tools:

Change is not just common in today's financial world; it is unavoidable. We have seen a transition that has taken the conventional banking industry from paper-laden offices to computerized platforms in a short period of time, with the Internet serving as the trigger. Kiyosaki's initial book stressed financial intelligence; nevertheless, in today's setting, this intelligence also involves comprehending and responding to these fast technological advances.

With a few taps, anybody with a smartphone can now access investing platforms, participate in peer-to-peer lending, or even manage their whole portfolio. Once a tiny and misunderstood subject, cryptocurrencies have risen as a powerful asset class. Blockchain technologies, for example, offer not just new currencies but also totally new methods to conduct contracts and transactions. These developments are democratizing financial possibilities and making them more accessible to a broader population.

These possibilities, however, bring with them obstacles. The abundance of tools and platforms available might be intimidating. Not all digital currencies will prosper, and not all technologically advanced investing platforms will last. The essence of current financial intelligence is distinguishing real possibilities from passing trends. It's no longer enough to recognize a solid real estate bargain or stock purchase; it's also important to comprehend the technical foundations that make an investment smart.

Furthermore, cybersecurity has emerged as a critical problem. Potential risks migrate online as transactions happen. Keeping one's assets safe in the digital environment is as important as any financial choice.

This emphasizes the need for lifelong learning. Financial seminars, webinars, online courses, and even podcasts may be quite beneficial. They provide insights into not just the "what" of the contemporary financial instrument but also the "why" and "how" of its operation. In today's world, a good investor is one who supplements their conventional financial knowledge with these current subtleties.

Understanding its Financial Implications

In the twenty-first century, the word 'job security' has taken on a new connotation. Careers are no longer linear, frequently with a single company or within a single sector. The gig economy is altering the basic fabric of work, spurred by technology breakthroughs.

Platforms such as Uber, Airbnb, and Fiverr have promoted the idea of short-term contracts or freelance employment replacing conventional full-time positions. For many, this provides incredible freedom and a plethora of chances. A person may drive in the morning, rent out a spare room in their home in the afternoon, and develop graphics at night.

The financial mechanics of gig labor, however, differ from those of typical employment. Income may be erratic, and benefits like health insurance or retirement contributions may be unavailable. This necessitates a new approach to financial planning and investment. It is critical for anyone working in the gig economy to grasp these disparities in order to ensure that they are not just earning but also safeguarding and expanding their profits.

Being a freelancer or a gig worker often entails being an entrepreneur. It entails selling one's services, customer management, and financial management. Investing in one's talents is essential not just to keep ahead of the competition but also to demand higher rates and ensure a steady income.

In essence, the gig economy epitomizes the ethos of the current financial landscape: it is dynamic and provides many options, but also requires a fresh and ongoing emphasis on learning and flexibility. Understanding the financial ramifications of the gig economy is becoming more important as the borders between work, entrepreneurship, and investment blur.

Financial Literacy in the Age of Information Overload

The internet-enabled world of today stands in sharp contrast to the comparatively simpler days of 1997 when Kiyosaki introduced readers to fundamental financial ideas. The sheer amount of knowledge at one's fingertips is both a blessing and a curse. While access to financial knowledge has never been simpler, filtering through this deluge of data to obtain useful and accurate insights may be difficult.

Because of the Internet's worldwide connection, happenings in one region of the globe may have an impact on financial markets all over the world. Consider how geopolitical events affect oil prices or how a tweet from a public person may influence stock market sentiment. In our interconnected world, knowing global events, cultures, and economies is critical to making educated financial decisions.

Furthermore, the growth of social media and influencer culture has provided a forum for a plethora of self-proclaimed financial experts. While many provide insightful information, others sell half-baked advice or personal agendas. Critical thinking and judgment are now more important than ever. In today's world, financial literacy is not just knowing money mechanics but also gaining the capacity to sift the wheat from the chaff when it comes to financial advice.

Furthermore, the democratization of finance implies that people are increasingly putting financial concerns into their own hands, bypassing conventional gatekeepers such as financial consultants. Platforms that provide commission-free trading, such as Robinhood, promote a do-it-yourself approach. While this is liberating, it also means that people suffer the brunt of their financial choices, making financial education and literacy not only desirable but also necessary.

However, in this information era, nothing is difficult. There are several resources accessible for people willing to devote time to continual learning. Online courses on a variety of financial subjects are available from universities and institutes. Platforms like Coursera and Udemy make top-tier financial courses more accessible, while podcasts and webinars provide bite-sized insights for the on-the-go person. Peer-to-peer learning platforms and forums enable beginners to benefit from the experiences and errors of seasoned investors.

Recommendations for resources and tools to stay informed.

Choosing the Right Financial Courses and E-Books

The notion of online education was in its early beginnings in the late 1990s. Today, the internet arena is brimming with financial courses, webinars, e-books, and other resources. The issue for the contemporary financial enthusiast or expert isn't always locating materials but rather picking the best ones from a sea of them.

The Internet's promise was to make knowledge easily accessible to everybody. It has surely fulfilled that promise but with one exception. Not all information is created equal, and due to the enormity of the Internet, high-quality resources often coexist alongside deceptive or mediocre material. As a result, the burden of discernment lies squarely on the individual.

Courses, for example, have grown in popularity as a means of gaining in-depth expertise on specialized subjects. Courses from colleges and institutions all around the globe are hosted on platforms like Coursera, Udemy, and edX. However, before enrolling, it is critical to investigate variables such as the instructor's qualifications, feedback from previous students, and the course content (Caucci, 2022). A well-chosen course may be transformational, providing insights that can be utilized immediately in real-world situations.

E-books, on the other hand, provide for the ease of reading at one's own speed. The popularity of e-readers and applications has grown much further. Financial e-books vary from introductory instructions to in-depth analysis of economic trends. The trick is to find reliable writers and publications. Reading sample chapters or reviews may often give insight into the content's quality.

Furthermore, it is critical to understand that learning is more than simply formal classes or books. Forums, blogs, podcasts, and even YouTube channels may be information gold mines. Platforms such as Reddit and Quora often offer debates in which experts share their viewpoints. Podcasts, because of their audio format, may be listened to during commutes, making them an effective learning tool. The necessity of confirming facts and cross-referencing material, as with any resource, cannot be stressed.

The digital era provides many paths for people interested in continual financial learning. However, with this wealth comes the responsibility of making wise decisions. One may genuinely utilize the power of the Internet to keep informed in the changing world of finance by improving one's selection skills, guaranteeing diversified sources of knowledge, and being open to different methods of learning.

Blending Traditional and Digital:

While the digital revolution has altered our access to knowledge, traditional means of learning and keeping informed should not be overlooked. They provide richness, human engagement, and tactile experiences that digital means may not.

Libraries, for example, continue to be knowledge repositories. The tactile experience of exploring bookshelves and reading tangible books has a distinct appeal. Furthermore, libraries often hold seminars, workshops, and conversations, which provide opportunities for face-to-face encounters with professionals and other fans. These seminars have the potential to spark spontaneous debates, provide networking opportunities, and provide a better grasp of issues.

Workshops and seminars, although seeming antiquated in comparison to modern internet webinars, give hands-on experiences. These events provide immediate interaction due to their participatory nature and real-time Q&A sessions. Practical activities, group discussions, and fast feedback ensure that participants have a thorough understanding of the subject at hand.

Even as we embrace digital technologies, we must acknowledge that human interactions bring about subtleties that may be overlooked in an online situation. Participating in debates, disputing points of view, and comprehending diverse points of view may help to expand one's knowledge.

Furthermore, despite the development of digital journalism, conventional newspapers and magazines continue to be vital providers of well-researched financial news and analysis. Their strict editing standards assure a certain amount of reliability.

The Art and Science of Financial Forecasting in the Digital Age

Financial forecasting was essentially the domain of economic specialists, seasoned stockbrokers, and financial institutions in Kiyosaki's day. Though successful at the time, their tactics were dependent on restricted data sources, slower communication methods, and long-established economic theories. Today's landscape is starkly different. The Internet has created a flood of real-time data, machine learning algorithms predict market moves, and communication is at light speed. However, with these gains comes the issue of distinguishing true signals from noise.

At its foundation, financial forecasting is an attempt to anticipate the future based on past and current facts. However, the data available now is extensive and diverse. From social media attitudes impacting stock prices to geopolitical events influencing global markets, the contemporary forecaster must take a variety of things into account. While data availability is a boon, it can also be a liability. Too much data might cause analytical paralysis or lead to incorrect conclusions if not properly evaluated.

The emergence of machine learning and artificial intelligence (AI) is one of the important breakthroughs assisting financial forecasting. These algorithms can swiftly evaluate large datasets, detecting patterns and abnormalities that human analysts would overlook. For example, AI systems may monitor news stories, financial data, and even Twitter feeds to evaluate market mood, offering previously inconceivable real-time information.

Despite this technical superiority, human intuition and knowledge remain unrivaled. A trend may be detected by a computer, but grasping the cultural, political, or social subtleties sometimes takes human intuition. Furthermore, history has demonstrated that markets are driven not just by facts but also by emotions, perceptions, and, at times, the unpredictable character of humans. As a result, although machines supply the power, human judgment directs the course.

For forecasters, there is also a growing focus on ongoing learning and flexibility. Strategies and approaches that were effective a decade ago may be outdated now. The contemporary financial expert must be ready to abandon outmoded approaches in favor of innovative methods. This might include taking online classes on new forecasting methods, attending seminars on global economic trends, or just networking with colleagues to share information.

Financial forecasting in the digital era is an art as well as a science. It's about matching robots' sheer computing capability with humans' nuanced knowledge. The ability to effectively foresee will be among the most sought-after abilities as the financial sector continues to grow, propelled by technology improvements and global interconnection.

Emphasizing adaptability as a key trait for financial success.

Overcoming Cognitive Biases in Investment Choices

Our brains, influenced by evolutionary processes and personal experiences, often include cognitive biases that might lead us astray from making the best financial choices. These biases, which range from the overconfidence effect to loss aversion, were likely less apparent in Kiyosaki's setting, but they are becoming more important in today's complicated world of finance. Understanding and recognizing these psychological hazards is critical for anybody seeking financial success.

Overconfidence, for example, maybe a two-edged sword. While it may motivate one to take chances and explore new routes, it may also cause one to underestimate possible consequences. Many newbie investors may assume they can outwit the market because of a few early victories or the tremendous quantity of information accessible on the Internet. However, seasoned professionals recognize that no one has a crystal ball and that investing with humility frequently pays well.

Another major cognitive bias is loss aversion, which is the propensity for people to favor avoiding losses over gaining similar benefits. This indicates that the psychological effect of losing $100 is greater than the joy of obtaining the same amount. Such biases might impair rational decision-making in a quickly changing financial environment, where new asset classes like cryptocurrencies can be volatile. Instead of reducing losses and reallocating resources to other potential initiatives, an investor may stick to a lost asset for too long, believing it will recover.

But it's not all doom and gloom. It is feasible to lessen the consequences of these biases by being aware of them and constantly educating oneself. Scenario planning, soliciting several perspectives, and taking measured risks after a comprehensive study are all tactics that might assist in this area. In summary, financial flexibility is about more than simply knowing markets; it is also about understanding oneself.

Financial Mentorship in the Age of Information Overload

The spread of the Internet and the democratization of financial knowledge has created an intriguing paradox: although information is more accessible than ever, the sheer amount of it may be overwhelming. This is where financial mentoring, a subject that resonates with the basic principles of "Rich Dad," becomes essential in the present setting.

The contrasting guidance from Kiyosaki's 'Rich Dad' and 'Poor Dad' gave important insights into wealth development and management in Kiyosaki's tale. In today's world of financial gurus, online courses, and investing forums, finding a trustworthy mentor might be like looking for a needle in a haystack. However, the significance of such counsel cannot be emphasized. A mentor may give context, filter out noise, and steer mentees toward solid financial choices based on their collected expertise and experience.

Furthermore, mentoring is about cultivating the proper mentality as much as providing information. In the world of finance, the value of perseverance, patience, and long-term vision is ageless. A successful mentor stresses these characteristics, ensuring that although their mentees use cutting-edge tools and techniques, they do so with a solid knowledge of fundamental financial concepts.

Financial mentoring is very important in networking. A strong mentor-mentee connection may result in introductions to industry insiders, suggestions for intriguing prospects, and insights into market intricacies. Finally, in a day where algorithms and AI-driven technologies dominate the financial conversation, the human touch of mentoring is as important as ever.

Balancing Digital Literacy with Traditional Financial Wisdom

The digital revolution has transformed how we connect, invest, and educate ourselves in the financial sector. The technologies at our disposal today, from blockchain's decentralized ledgers to AI-driven robo-advisors, would have looked extraterrestrial in Kiyosaki's 1997 scenario. However, while we rush to embrace these new wonders, there is an urgent need to root ourselves in conventional financial thinking.

The digital environment entices with the promise of instant riches. The spectacular climbs (and dips) of cryptocurrencies attest to this fascination. They've democratized wealth creation, allowing ordinary people to observe portfolio development that would have previously taken years, if not decades. However, this potential for quick gain is accompanied by an equal, if not larger, danger of loss. Traditional concepts like diversification, long-term planning, and risk assessment may easily be overlooked in the cloud of these digital gold rushes.

It is here that the lessons of the past, many of which may be found in the pages of Kiyosaki's original text, become crucial. They act as an anchor, reminding us that although technologies and trends change, some fundamental values do not. For example, the age-old adage "don't put all your eggs in one basket" still applies, even if those baskets are now digital wallets or online investing platforms.

Furthermore, although today's information overload is powerful, it may also lead to analytical paralysis. Endless charts, graphs, and real-time updates at our fingertips may encourage a hyperactive trading attitude, driving people to make rash judgments based on short-term market changes. The conventional knowledge of patience and seeing investments as long-term commitments is essential in this situation.

However, ignoring contemporary technologies in favor of strictly conventional ways is not the answer. In today's financial economy, digital literacy is critical. The balance that contemporary investors should aim for is understanding how to harness technology while also acknowledging its limits and possible hazards. For example, although utilizing robo-advisors for portfolio management might be beneficial, blind reliance without comprehending the underlying algorithms can be harmful.

Chapter 9

Success Stories

The road to financial freedom is, as usual, fraught with difficulties. The complicated mazes of contemporary finance may be intimidating for many people. Here comes the importance of success tales. These triumphant, resilient, and innovative stories serve as guiding beacons in the thick jungle of financial choices, inspiring, educating, and encouraging folks navigating today's economic environment.

To begin with, success tales humanize financial ideas. They make abstract concepts more approachable by transforming them into relatable tales. When readers hear about someone who, in a situation similar to their own, created a lucrative route by harnessing technologies such as robo-advisors, bitcoin, or digital real estate platforms, it becomes simpler for them to see their own success. It's an ancient adage: "If they can do it, so can"

Furthermore, these tales often go into the errors and setbacks faced along the way. This is priceless for today's financial enthusiast. By learning the problems that others have encountered, individuals may proceed with care, making educated choices that reduce risk. These cautionary warnings inside success stories are often as valuable as the victories.

Furthermore, success tales serve as proof of the effectiveness of current financial instruments and tactics. Reading about a content creator who converted from regular employment to financial independence using online platforms or from a person who created money by managing the crypto market wisely gives actual evidence. It strengthens trust in modern procedures and dispels many misconceptions and fears.

Success stories serve as updated blueprints in a continually changing environment where yesterday's standards might be today's archaisms. They highlight how people are adapting, inventing, and prospering in the face of economic upheaval. They are communal narratives of adaptation, resilience, and invention in the face of current difficulties, not simply stories of individual victory.

Success stories are really about the human spirit and drive. They have an emotional impact, inspiring hope and encouraging aspiration. They remind readers that success is feasible despite the difficulties of today's financial environment. They promote the concept that with the correct information, skills, and mentality, anybody can create a path to financial success.

Success stories are more than simply triumphant narratives. They are catalysts that stimulate action, blueprints that direct attempts, and reassurances that success, even in this sophisticated arena, is within reach in the current financial environment. They are definitely an important aspect of financial discourse, deserving of a presence in any modern financial handbook.

Real-life case studies of financial success in the modern era:

Analyzing the Strategy of Jeff Bezos

When examining the trend of financial success stories in the contemporary period, one cannot ignore Jeff Bezos' remarkable climb. Bezos, the founder of Amazon, developed a basic online bookshop into one of the world's most powerful enterprises. So, what can hopefuls learn from his experience?

Bezos' plan was always long-term in nature. He was recognized for putting client pleasure above quick earnings, which seemed illogical at the time. Amazon went beyond books by reinvesting money in the firm, establishing roots in industries ranging from retail to cloud computing.

Risk-taking was central to much of Bezos' approach. He used a "fail fast" attitude when venturing into areas where Amazon had no previous knowledge. Projects like the Fire Phone were unsuccessful, but the principles learned were used by more successful enterprises like Alexa and Echo.

Bezos recognized the need for scalability in the digital era. Amazon Web Services (AWS), an internal cloud platform, has been made available to external customers. It is now a major profit generator for Amazon, demonstrating Bezos' vision of diversifying revenue sources (Chaffey, 2023).

In essence, Bezos' approach has been to imagine a distant future and methodically guide the ship in that direction, unafraid of occasional setbacks. It demonstrates the need for adaptation, forethought, and constant concentration in contemporary financial success.

Analyzing the Strategy of Mark Zuckerberg

Mark Zuckerberg's rise from a Harvard dorm room to the leadership of one of the world's most powerful internet businesses, Facebook, provides fascinating insights into contemporary financial success. What were Zuckerberg's motivations, and how may they be used today?

Zuckerberg had an excellent awareness of market gaps from the start. Recognizing the human need for connection,

Facebook was created as a reflection of our innate urge to belong, not only as a social network. This user-centric approach formed the foundation of Facebook's development.

Adaptability was also highlighted by Zuckerberg. As mobile technology started to take off, he made certain that Facebook was at the forefront of this transformation. His purchase of Instagram, while it was only a fledgling platform, demonstrated his intuition about where digital trends were headed.

However, Zuckerberg's plan was more than simply capturing the moment; it was also about ongoing innovation. While Facebook started as a social networking platform, it quickly broadened its scope, diving into virtual reality with Oculus and even digital currency efforts like Libra.

His approach to partnerships and acquisitions, such as WhatsApp and Oculus, reveals a deep awareness of combining capabilities, resulting in many development opportunities.

Reflecting on Zuckerberg's trajectory, it's clear that contemporary success requires more than simply building a product; it's also about understanding its function in a bigger ecosystem. It's about anticipating change, being adaptive, and, most importantly, staying fiercely imaginative in the face of adversity (Case Study on Mark Zuckerberg | Researchomatic, 2022).

Analyzing the Strategy of Elon Musk

Elon Musk stands out in the pantheon of contemporary financial giants as a creative entrepreneur whose initiatives range from electric autos to space exploration. His business style provides a multitude of insights for people pursuing financial success in the modern day.

Elon Musk's approach is often based on disrupting the status quo. The vehicle business was heavily established in gasoline-driven paradigms when he co-founded Tesla. Musk's vision of an electric future included not just environmental awareness but also demonstrating electric automobiles as better in performance and economy. Tesla has risen to the top of the vehicle market because of its commitment to iterative design and continuous development.

Another of Musk's enterprises, SpaceX, has a similar attitude of questioning conventional wisdom. Musk not only transformed the cost structure of space missions by bringing reusability in rocketry, but he also laid forth a broader vision: populating Mars as a backup for mankind.

Musk's endeavors into solar energy (SolarCity), subterranean transportation (The Boring Company), and brain-machine interfaces (Neuralink) demonstrate a common trend. Musk finds businesses that are ripe for disruption, assembles a team of elite specialists, and tirelessly pursues an ambitious idea. His philosophy is based on disruptive innovation rather than gradual improvement (Dhiraj, 2021).

While opponents sometimes refer to Musk's bold statements and timeframes, his dedication to the long-term goal, paired with his ability to adapt and pivot, distinguishes him as a model of contemporary financial success.

Analyzing the Strategy of Ricardo Salinas Pliego

Mexican business mogul Ricardo Salinas Pliego has carved himself a unique position in the Latin American corporate scene. Pliego's strategic choices as the founder and chairman of Grupo Salinas provide a deep dive into developing and maintaining conglomerates in emerging nations.

Pliego's early triumphs were in retail and consumer goods, but he showed a sharp eye for moving into industries that cater to the rising requirements of a developing middle class. His forays into telecoms with TV Azteca and mobile communications with Unefon were opportune, tapping into the Mexican population's media consumption patterns and connection demands.

Pliego's approach with Banco Azteca also included financial inclusion. Recognizing that conventional banks were underserving a big portion of the Latin American population, he used his retail network to provide banking services, creating a paradigm change in how financial services were accessible in the area.

Pliego's approach often centered on finding market gaps and exploiting existing infrastructure to fill them (Munoz, 2019). Furthermore, his faith in the potential of new technology is shown in his positive outlook on cryptocurrencies, which he sees as a viable alternative to established financial institutions.

In short, Ricardo Salinas Pliego's journey emphasizes the need for adaptation, knowing local idiosyncrasies, and anticipating technological advances, all of which are characteristics of financial success in the present globalized world.

Conclusion

We traveled through the convoluted labyrinth of contemporary finance in the previous pages, finding similarities with the ideas popularized by Robert Kiyosaki in 1997's "Rich Dad, Poor Dad." However, as we travel these pathways of financial wisdom, we are painfully conscious of the profoundly transformed environment around us—a world in which technology not only supports but also dictates our financial choices.

The internet's pervasiveness has undeniably transformed our access to financial information. We are no longer constrained by the constraints of conventional banking, investing, and financial consulting. Today, we can access a complete array of financial products, ranging from investing applications to cryptocurrency wallets, with the touch of a mouse. Individuals have been empowered and required to become stewards of their own financial destiny as a result of this democratization.

While the principles of investing, accumulating wealth, and financial literacy are timeless, their implementation has changed. We live in a world where cryptocurrencies, which were long considered a niche interest, are now seriously considered potential cornerstones of global finance. Similarly, real estate, a once-exclusive domain, is now open to everybody thanks to innovations like property crowdfunding.

These great improvements, however, are not without complications. The contemporary investor, entrepreneur, or wage worker faces a slew of options, each more complex than the last. The use of derivatives, ETFs, and algorithmic trading is just the tip of the iceberg. To navigate this complex environment, a renewed focus on financial literacy becomes not just useful but also necessary.

Furthermore, our connection with money has undergone a metamorphosis. The emotions, attitudes, and deeply held ideas that we identify with money and income have grown in breadth. With its rapid satisfaction and continual comparisons, the digital era has heightened feelings such as FOMO (Fear of Missing Out) and magnified the contradiction between scarcity and abundance mindsets. Recognizing and controlling these psychological components is just as important as learning the technical parts of money.

Diversifying income sources is no longer a pipe dream for many people in this day and age. From content production to affiliate marketing, the digital sphere provides a plethora of options, each with its own set of benefits and obstacles.

Real estate, an evergreen investment, has undergone its own metamorphosis. The modern investor must be as knowledgeable about short-term rental dynamics as they are about conventional property investing. Technology, in this and other domains, is a double-edged sword, providing improved managerial capabilities but also altering market dynamics in unexpected ways.

Perhaps the most important takeaway from this investigation is the critical role of adaptation. The financial world will continue to evolve as a result of technological breakthroughs, global events, and shifting human behavior. To prosper in it, one must not just be knowledgeable but also eager to learn, change, and adapt on a regular basis.

Reflecting on the journeys of individuals like Jeff Bezos, Mark Zuckerberg, Elon Musk, and Riccardo Salinas Pliego, it is clear that, although the essential elements of financial wisdom remain intact, their implementation in the current world requires a sophisticated knowledge and a dynamic approach.

While borrowing inspiration from a classic, this book seeks to serve as a guide for the current reader. A handbook that, although founded in timeless knowledge, looks forward to assisting readers in navigating the ever-changing environment of the current financial world.

References

Munoz, S. (2019, March 3). *Ricardo Salinas Pliego - Los Angeles Times*. Los Angeles Times. https://www.latimes.com/archives/la-xpm-1998-jul-12-op-2966-story.html

Case Study On Mark Zuckerberg | Researchomatic. (n.d.). https://www.researchomatic.com/Case-Study-On-Mark-Zuckerberg-47210.html

T. (n.d.). *The Importance of Being a Continuous Learner for Financial Professionals*. Nasdaq. https://www.nasdaq.com/articles/the-importance-of-being-a-continuous-learner-for-financial-professionals

Caucci, S. (2022, June 17). *Importance of Continuous Learning in Finance Manager Training*. 1Huddle. https://1huddle.co/blog/learning-in-finance-sector/

McCormick, K. (2023, July 18). *40+ Easy & Effective Real Estate Marketing Ideas [Updated!]*. WordStream. https://www.wordstream.com/blog/ws/2015/04/16/real-estate-marketing

Emerging Trends in Real Estate 2023. (n.d.). PwC. https://www.pwc.com/us/en/industries/financial-services/asset-wealth-management/real-estate/emerging-trends-in-real-estate.html

M. (2023, May 17). *30 Ways to Diversify Your Income (Multiple Parallel Revenue Streams)*. Business Advisor. https://mariopeshev.com/diversify-income-revenue-streams/

Herrick, J. (2023, September 6). *How to Diversify Income Streams for Long-Term Financial Growth*. Entrepreneur. https://www.entrepreneur.com/money-finance/how-to-diversify-income-streams-for-long-term-financial/458332#:~:text=By%20diversifying%20income%20streams%2C%20you,tapping%20into%20previously%20untapped%20markets.

Rucker, J. (2023, June 23). *How emotions play a role in managing your money*. Financial Insights for Individuals and Businesses. https://blog.umb.com/personal-banking-tips-emotions-of-money-management-1/

The Psychology of Money By Morgan Housel - StudentStore.pk. (2023, September 18). StudentStore.pk. https://studentstore.pk/book/the-psychology-of-money-by-morgan-housel/

The Psychology of Money: Timeless lessons on wealth, greed, and happiness: Housel, Morgan: 9780857197689: Amazon.com: Books. (n.d.). https://www.amazon.com/Psychology-Money-Timeless-lessons-happiness/dp/0857197681

H. (n.d.). *Complexity in Financial Markets*. Hindawi. https://www.hindawi.com/journals/complexity/si/18726 8/

Understanding the investment landscape | Quilter Cheviot. (n.d.). www.quiltercheviot.com. https://www.quiltercheviot.com/news-and-views/women-and-investing/understanding-the-investment-landscape/

What is the impact of technology on financial services? | HCLTech. (n.d.). https://www.hcltech.com/technology-qa/what-is-the-impact-of-technology-on-financial-services

Bilyk, I. (2023, August 21). *The Role of Technology in Financial Services: The Best FinTech Solutions*. YouTeam. https://youteam.io/blog/the-role-of-technology-in-financial-services/#:~:text=Technology%20in%20financial%20se rvices%20has,cybersecurity%20solutions%2C%20and% 20digital%20banking.

Dhiraj, A. B. (2021, November 3). *Elon Musk: A Case Study of The World's Richest, Influential, And Most Controversial Man*. CEOWORLD Magazine. https://ceoworld.biz/2021/11/03/elon-musk-a-case-study-of-the-worlds-richest-influential-and-most-controversial-man/

Chaffey, D. (2023, February 27). *Amazon marketing strategy business case study | Smart Insights*. Smart Insights. https://www.smartinsights.com/digital-marketing-strategy/online-business-revenue-models/amazon-case-study/